GAME IN SEASON
The Orvis Cookbook

GAME IN SEASON
The Orvis Cookbook

by Romi Perkins
Introduction by Gene Hill

Illustrated by Judy Sgantas

NICK LYONS BOOKS

WINCHESTER PRESS
An Imprint of New Century Publishers

With admiration and love,
I dedicate this book
to Jessie Hill.

Printed in the United States of America

10 9 8 7 6 5 4 3 2

Produced by: Nick Lyons Books
             31 West 21 Street
             New York, NY 10010

Published and distributed by: New Century Publishers
                               220 Old New Brunswick Road
                               Piscataway, NJ 08854

Library of Congress Cataloging in Publication Data

Perkins, Romi.
   Game in season.

   Includes index.
   1. Cookery (Game) 2. Cookery (Fish) 3. Menus.
I. Title.
TX751.P46 1986   641.6'91   86–18036
ISBN 0–8329–0447–3

CONTENTS

ACKNOWLEDGMENTS

Early on in my life, my parents set standards for cooking and eating for which I am ardently grateful. There was never even a jar of peanut butter in the house, much less any of the lower tier of edibles known as junk food.

Now that I have grown up healthy as a horse (and use peanut butter in my salad dressing on occasion), I wish to thank my intrepid and beloved husband, Leigh Perkins, who introduced me to the pleasures and rigors of fishing and hunting—year in and year out, around the world. His passion for properly cooked game is matched only by his devotion to the birds and fish themselves, and to maintaining their habitat.

I want to express my dedication to the memory of his mother, Katharine Haskell Perkins, who rarely set foot in a kitchen, but whose adeptness as a sportswoman always awed me and eluded my efforts at emulation. She set high standards as a hostess, and in this was aided by her cook of forty-five years, Jessie Hill. Jessie, in her gentle way, has taught three generations of the Perkins family how to prepare delectable game for the table.

Next, my loving appreciation to two good cooks, Penelope Mesic and Melissa Perkins, my daughters, who have helped me with their suggestions, good taste, and enthusiasm.

I add my gratitude to the many cooks I have met at home and in our travels who have served memorable meals and shared cooking experience with me. Unfortunately, I don't even know all their names: Deep Annand's chef in Uttar Pradesh; the chef at the Captain Cook Hotel on Christmas Island; the cook at Underley Grange, Lancashire, England.

Recognition is due to Bill Cheney for the cover

photograph; Dick Davis, wild-food gatherer *par excellence*, Barbara Dupree, my dear sister, who prompted me to adapt Madame Begue's Creamed Soda Crackers; Pamela Grosscup, Cleveland, Ohio, my cooking teacher and source of many recipes and much inspiration; Gene Hill, for his wonderful foreword, more readable than the body of most texts; Dr. Cyril J. Jones, Brooklyn, New York. Profound thanks to Gene McAvoy, Visiting Art Director and cultural hero from Los Angeles, California; Richard E. McConnell, Greenwich, Connecticut; Tish North, Head Chef for Safari South, Botswana; Jo Reynolds of Gates Mills, Ohio, one of the best cooks I know; Anthea and John Russell, charming hosts and excellent cooks, Nether Wallop Mill, Hampshire, England; Señora Gonzales and Steve at Boca Paila, Yucatán; and Ziggie Fjeldsted, guide and gravlax master from Iceland.

I am especially grateful to my tasters and testers: Nancy Aitken, Greg Comar, Ann Dupree, Stephanie Jacob, and Marsha Norman.

For his encouragement, low-pressure strategy, and judicious advice, my sense of obligation to Nick Lyons is boundless.

ROMI M. PERKINS
Battenkill Farm
Manchester, Vermont
February 1986

FOREWORD

There are several reasons why I wanted to do this foreword to Romi's cookbook. One is that she's a very witty person (you'll discover that for yourself), and I very much enjoy her company. Another reason is that this is a small way for me to further pay obeisance for the meals I've enjoyed at her table and, most importantly, I might get invited back for Chapter 9, Chapter 33, and/or Chapter 4.

Some of my favorite reading is larded away in good cookbooks. A good cook, by my definition, is a cheerful artisan who not only loves and respects the art he or she is gifted with, but also manages to spread an aura of delight that is the critical spice for any gathering at the table. Romi's kitchen has all of that, abundantly. She does this without visible effort or strain and I have had the feeling, when observing Romi cook, that I might be watching Landseer do a landscape while fooling with the dog with his free hand and chatting amiably about the prospects for the coming bird season, and all the time a marvel is appearing with mysterious ease—as it always does when guided by the hand of genius.

When one learns anything he tends to favor certain elements of the education. A shooter becomes fond of a light English twelve bore; it is his instrument and he performs well with it. A fisherman will come to prefer a particular circumstance—a tarpon flat with its mind-stretching vistas of a curling-away horizon and the soaring frigate birds, or perhaps the muted coziness of a New England trout stream and the hidden piping of a thrush or cardinal. An eater too will come to his forte—and since it parallels my dedication, I am an eager and heavy indulger in the fruits of my pastime, game and fish.

As is typical of the gourmand (one of my favorite

food writers, the late A. J. Leibling, said that it was impossible to like food if you did not like a lot of it; *gourmet* was therefore a snob word and a silly one), I am either teetering on the edge of indigestion or on a diet. I am in envy and awe of one of the legends of the table, the name slips my mind at the moment, who, when offered one of those mini-catalog menus, leafed through it pensively, closed it, and handed it back to the waiter saying, "I see nothing to object to." This is how I feel having leafed through Romi Perkins's work for the nth time, trying to remember what I have left in the way of doves or quail or salmon or ducks in the freezer.

These are, in the main, meals for people who like to eat. Romi knows game cooking as well as anyone —and well she might, being both a fine shot and fisherman, and a traveler to every known cranny in the world with few inhibitions about eating the local fare, whatever it might be. She is an imaginative and joyous and generous cook, which, as you can see, I deeply appreciate. On the other hand, she has written the lovely and witty, "It all makes one feel so sorry for Ernest Hemingway's characters; they obviously went into the bush with the wrong outfitters. Francis Macomber's wife would have gained ten pounds, happily, and Death would have gotten his bicycle stuck in the sand just outside the mess tent." That's the sort of thing that makes me jealous!

This is, as you will happily discover, that rare and precious blend of good things for both the stomach and the mind. My copy will shortly bear the marks of the well used. As my favorite hunting and fishing books accumulate droplets of oil and page markers of broken-hook flies, this book will wear wineglass circles and sport feathers for page markers.

I'll never be as good a cook as Romi—but we do share a common trait or two in the kitchen: the ability to step carefully over three or four dogs and the habit of wiping our hands on the seat of our hunting pants.

GENE HILL
Robinwood Farm
Pennington, New Jersey

2

INTRODUCTION

This is not a nice, normal, lavishly illustrated cocktail-table cookbook. It has a few recipes for some excruciatingly time-consuming dishes (one is for an apple pie.) It also has some of the quickest cookery ever devised. It advocates using the most expensive meat thermometer in the world, and suggests buying a three-hundred-and-fifty-dollar duck press. But to keep it in balance, it incorporates leftovers from one meal to create an appealing future meal. The Orvis Meat Thermicator will pay for itself in a year by helping to prevent you from ruining fifty-dollar roasts or charcoal-grilled steaks, not to mention five-hundred-dollar ducks (if you belong to a duck club or run a plantation, you know I'm not exaggerating).

This book tries to temper the need for Erma Bombeck's wonderful recipe for Bombeck Garbage. She included it in an introduction to a recent cookbook. It featured saving every little dab of leftovers in small foil-covered containers and curing them for two weeks in the refrigerator. The result, of course, is familiar to us all.

If you can't use this as a cookbook, try using it as a rudimentary travel guide to find out what part of the world you could be in at given times, should you want to fish and shoot for an uninterrupted year.

It should be mentioned that there are many recipes included that do not feature game, and most can be prepared with domestically raised birds and fish that are readily available the year round.

The wild game in your freezer represents a considerable effort by dedicated sportsmen's groups, privately funded organizations, individuals, and government agencies who work and contribute millions of dollars annually to maintain wildlife habitat. Wild game is precious and it is a grave error, not to say a sin, to ruin it in the kitchen by overcooking.

Many recipes in game cookbooks end with a phrase such as "cook until done," or "cook until tender." Ignore all such advice and take it as an axiom that accuracy in cooking time is essential in preparing any food, but particularly in cooking game or fish.

If you weren't fortunate enough to have grown up with a superb game cook you could learn from, you can buy an instrument that will instantly tell you the internal temperature, or degree of doneness, in anything you are cooking, by whatever method. For detailed information about this sophisticated surrogate chef cum instructor, see the Appendix. Warning: Do not expect the same results with ordinary meat thermometers. I will describe other methods that can be used to determine when meat or fish are properly cooked, but none is as easy, foolproof, and quick as using this thermocouple wonder.

From many years of traveling, shooting, fishing, and dining in many parts of the world, this is a small part of what I have brought back. My thought in presenting it is from an essay by Francis Bacon: "When a traveler returneth home, let him not leave the countries where he hath traveled altogether behind him."

ONE

HAPPY NEW YEAR AND GOOD LUCK!

January

ROAST CANADA GOOSE

◆

BUTTERNUT SQUASH AND CHESTNUT PURÉE

◆

CHOUCROUTE WITH APPLES AND JUNIPER BERRIES

◆

BUENA VISTA ZINFANDEL

◆

BIBB LETTUCE WITH MUSTARD AND SWEET CREAM DRESSING

◆

CRANBERRY ICE CREAM

Every culture has its good-luck foods. Cannibals eat the hearts of their slain enemies. The immaculate and thrifty Swiss, in a gesture that would be unthinkable on any day except New Year's, eat whipped cream, making sure to dump some on the floor to guarantee abundance in the coming year. Austrians eat pink marzipan pigs, reflecting ancient beliefs that fish and pork symbolize a bounteous morrow. In the American South, black-eyed peas, as prepared in Hoppin' John, with hog jowl and rice, work their magic for the new year. A Creole dish made with red beans and rice, ham hocks and vegetables, has helped countless Louisiana natives face the coming year with high hopes; if collard greens or cabbage are added, the likelihood of green folding money coming one's way is greatly increased. In addition to eating stuffed cabbage and sauerkraut, Hungarian-Americans in Cleveland, Ohio, improve their odds by holding a silver dollar in their hands at five minutes to midnight.

Polish and Swedish descendants favor creamed herring; Norwegians gobble up creamed codfish or poached salmon. Italians feature lentils with spiced sausage, each round legume representing a coin. Greek-Americans celebrate St. Basil's Day along with New Year's Day and they bake a special cake called *vasiloppita* (flavored with aniseed, lemon, and orange), and hide a lucky coin inside.

With all this tradition involved, it would be downright foolish to whomp up a batch of Alligator Tail with Plantation Sauce for New Year's Day dinner and expect to make it through the coming year. Now you have no excuse, because this book is arranged to suggest what you can do in twelve months if you could take a year away from work, had an unlimited budget, and wanted to fish, hunt, and dine your way around the world. Now, eat your nize sauerkraut, and good luck to you!

Roast Canada Goose

The average weight of a Canada gander is 9 to 9½ pounds, although this can go up to 14 pounds easily, and some specimens may go up to 20 pounds. The goose averages 1 or 2 pounds lighter, on the average. The carcass should be hung under refrigeration (or outside at about 40°) for 5 to 6 days, in the feathers. (For instruction on cleaning and plucking, see Appendix.)

Preheat oven to 350°.

Take an average-sized, table-ready goose and stuff the cavity with 3 Granny Smith apples, cut into quarters, and 2 medium-sized onions, peeled and halved (add more apples and onions if goose is larger). Place the bird in an open roasting pan with ½ cup water. Bake approximately 8 minutes per pound. If the bird is 9 pounds *dressed weight*, that means 1 hour and 12 minutes.

After baking, internal temperature should be 130° to 150°. The goose will be tender and moist at 130°, firmer and drier at 150°. (It will get tougher, bordering on inedible the further it gets over 150°.) If you don't have a Thermicator, which tells you the internal temperature instantly, slide a sharp, thin knife down along the breastbone and peer inside. The flesh should be deep pink, fading to lighter pink and brown toward the outside. Remove the goose from the oven and allow it to stand at least 15 minutes before carving.

Discard the apples and onions before serving. If you want to stuff the bird, make a dressing from the basic recipe as for Roast Wild Turkey (*which see*).

Butternut Squash and Chestnut Purée

2 large butternut squash
½ pound raw chestnuts,
    blanched and peeled, or one
    32-ounce can prepared whole
    chestnuts (1 pound raw
    equals about 2½ cups peeled
    chestnuts. It's a chore to peel
    them, but this dish is better
    if they are fresh.)
3 stalks celery, cut roughly
2 cups canned beef bouillon
4 fresh parsley sprigs
1 medium onion, sliced
3 carrots, peeled and roughly
    cut into rounds
1 bay leaf
2 sprigs fresh thyme or ⅛
    teaspoon dried thyme
6 tablespoons softened butter
¼ cup heavy cream
2 teaspoons salt, with freshly
    ground pepper to taste added
2 tablespoons chopped parsley
    for garnish

If using fresh chestnuts, peel two ⅛-inch strips of shell in an X pattern on one side of each chestnut. Place them in a large heavy-bottomed saucepan, cover with cold water, bring to a boil, and boil 1 minute. Remove from heat, then, with a slotted spoon dip the chestnuts out of the water 2 or 3 at a time and peel off the shells and inner skins. Set aside any recalcitrant chestnuts. Drop these into boiling water for another minute, then peel them one by one. The peeling motion must be continuous, and done while the chestnuts are still warm.

Now put the peeled chestnuts into a heavy-bottomed saucepan with the carrots, celery, onion, and a *bouquet garni* of parsley, bay leaf, and thyme. Cover with the bouillon, adding water if necessary to cover. Bring to a boil, lower the heat and simmer for 45 to 60 minutes, or until the chestnuts are soft but not mushy.

Remove from the heat and drain, reserving the liquid. Discard the bay leaf and purée the chestnuts and vegetables by putting them through a food mill or food processor with a steel blade. Remove to a large bowl and set aside.

Meanwhile, peel, halve, and seed the squash. Cut into chunks and boil in a small amount of water for approximately 15 to 20 minutes, or until tender and easily pierced with a fork. Remove from the heat, drain, discard the liquid, and purée in batches. Add this to the bowl containing the puréed chestnuts.

If using canned chestnuts, simmer only the vegetables and *bouquet garni* in the bouillon for approximately 10 to 15 minutes. When the vegetables are almost soft, drop in the canned chestnuts, drained, and simmer for another 5 minutes. Remove from the heat and drain, saving the liquid. Discard the bay leaf. Purée the chestnuts and vegetables in batches and combine them with the puréed squash, as above.

Beat in the butter and half of the cream. Add the salt and pepper. If the purée is too thick, add some more of the cream or use some of the reserved bouillon. The mixture should be the consistency of mashed potatoes.

This recipe can be made ahead to this point and refrigerated with a cover of foil or plastic wrap. A little more than a half hour before you want to serve it, preheat the oven to 350°. Place the purée in a deep ovenproof casserole or soufflé dish. Cover with the lid or foil and place in a roasting pan. Pour boiling water into the pan to a level halfway up the sides of the casserole. Bake for 25 to 30 minutes. Serve in the casserole or soufflé dish with chopped parsley sprinkled around the edges.

Chestnuts are often used with turkey, goose, venison, and wild duck, but always seem almost too rich. The squash and chestnut flavors blend well and are an excellent contrast to the accompanying good-luck sauerkraut dish.

Happy New Year and Good Luck!

Choucroute with Apples and Juniper Berries

SERVES 8 TO 10

1 tablespoon chopped fresh dill, or 1 teaspoon dried dillweed
4 parsley sprigs
Pinch of caraway seed
2 bay leaves
8 juniper berries, crushed with mortar and pestle with 6 peppercorns
3 pounds fresh sauerkraut
2 cups finely chopped onions
3 cloves garlic, peeled and put through a garlic press
2 large Granny Smith apples, peeled, cored, and chopped
4 carrots, peeled and chopped
1 parsnip, peeled and chopped
¼ cup gin
1 cup Riesling wine
1 can chicken consommé, or better yet, 1 cup homemade chicken stock
1 pound lean salt pork
Salt and freshly ground black pepper
4 shelled walnuts

Tie the dill, parsley, caraway, bay, juniper and peppercorns into a piece of clean cheesecloth, so that you can remove them easily later.

Preheat oven to 325°.

Roughly cube the salt pork to ½-inch squares and brown in a large skillet. Drain on paper towels. Pour off all but 1 tablespoon of the rendered fat and add the onions, garlic, carrots, and parsnip. Sauté for 7 or 8 minutes, add the apples, and continue cooking until the vegetables are soft. Add the sauerkraut, mix well, and remove from the heat. Add the gin and wine and mix well.

Put half the sauerkraut mixture into a large casserole with a lid. Add the salt pork and the *bouquet garni*. Cover with the remaining half of the sauerkraut. Sprinkle the shelled walnuts on top. (They will prevent the sauerkraut smell from permeating your house.) Put the lid on and bake for 2 hours.

Remove from the oven, cool, and refrigerate overnight or for 2 or 3 days until you want to serve it.

A little more than 3 hours before serving, preheat the oven to 275° and bake the casserole very slowly for 3 hours. Don't forget to remove the cheesecloth bag of herbs and if you can't find the walnuts, don't worry—they taste good. Serve in a deep bowl or from the casserole. It is to be hoped you will have leftovers; this recipe is even better reheated the next day.

This dish will be much more flavorful if it is made at least 1 day ahead and cooked for just 2 hours, then cooled, refrigerated overnight, and reheated for 3 hours at low heat the day of serving. It can, however, be cooked for the full 5 hours on one day; just lower the heat to 275° for the final 3 hours.

Bibb Lettuce Salad with Mustard and Sweet Cream Dressing

SERVES 8

8 small heads Bibb lettuce, washed and dried

DRESSING

Mix the mustard, lemon juice, and salt together in a small bowl. Be sure all the lumps of mustard are dissolved. Pour in both measures of cream while whisking, and add freshly ground pepper to taste. Pour sparingly over the crisp greens and serve immediately.

½ cup light cream (18 percent)
¼ cup whipping cream
1 teaspoon dry mustard
Juice of 1 lemon
Scant ½ teaspoon salt and freshly ground pepper to taste

Happy New Year and Good Luck!

Cranberry Ice Cream

2 cups fresh cranberries
¾ cup water
1 cup sugar
Grated peel of 1 lemon
3 tablespoons lemon juice
¼ teaspoon freshly ground
  nutmeg
¼ teaspoon cinnamon
2 cups milk
1 cup heavy cream

Rinse the cranberries, place them in a heavy-bottomed saucepan with the water and the lemon peel, and bring to a boil. Lower the heat and simmer until the berries start popping open (about 7 minutes). Remove from the heat and put through a food mill or sieve (use a wooden spoon). If you use a food processor to purée the berries, you will have to put the purée through a sieve to remove the skins and any seeds or stems.

Place the purée in the saucepan, add the lemon juice and sugar, set over low heat and stir until the sugar dissolves. Remove from the heat and mix in the cinnamon and nutmeg. Cool. Add the milk, mix well, and refrigerate for 1 hour.

Beat the heavy cream until stiff, and fold it carefully into the cranberry mixture. Pour this into the chilled canister of your ice cream machine and freeze according to manufacturer's directions.

This ice cream is fresh and tart, but creamy. If you have any Highbush Cranberry Sauce (which see), make this dessert with it. Use two cups of the prepared sauce, mix with the milk, chill, and fold in the whipped cream before freezing. You'll be able to have some of this delicious ice cream in the middle of next summer if you make a supply of cranberry sauce this fall. It's a shame not to eat it more than once a year.

TWO

DO LOOK A GIFT HAUNCH IN THE MOUTH

January

SMOKED VENISON HAUNCH

◆

POTATO-TURNIP FLAN

◆

SPINACH SOUFFLÉ IN TOMATO HALVES

◆

HEARTS OF PALM SALAD

◆

CHAPPELLET NAPA VALLEY CABERNET SAUVIGNON

◆

APPLESAUCE TARTS

Smoked Venison Haunch

We do not do any deer hunting, but we do enjoy a venison dinner. We're fortunate to have some friends who hunt on our place and then drop off some venison. Perhaps you have an acquaintance who loves to hunt deer but who ties the buck to his fender and drives around town for 2 or 3 days showing it off. Firmly resist any offers of deer meat from him—it will be bad venison. It is important that the deer be skinned immediately after, or at least the same day, it has been killed. The carcass should be hung in a meat locker at 40° for 10 days to 2 weeks. Only then can you expect it to be the delicious treat it should be. If you have dogs, they might not object to deer meat that has been mishandled, but if you have no dogs, tell your deer-hunting acquaintance that you have just turned vegetarian, no thank you very much.

Assuming that you are the possessor of a haunch that has been skinned and hung properly, take it out to your smoker and make sure that it fits under the lid. Saw the shank end of the bone off if it doesn't. Light a charcoal fire in the bottom of the smoker. Fill the water pan that fits over the coals. Put a small piece of hickory wood into it to soak. Set aside.

In about 15 minutes, when the fire is well established, drop the wet piece of hickory wood into the coals. Place the pan of water over the coals, put the grill in place, and put the venison on the grill. Cover with the lid and start preparing the rest of the dinner.

Cooking the meat will probably take 2 hours, but this will vary depending upon the ambient temperature and the amount and type of charcoal used. Check on it every hour. The internal temperature should be 130° to 140° when it is done. It will be moist and firm, deep pink on the inside, lighter pink on the outside.

If the outside air temperature is between 45° and 65°, it *is* possible to start the fire in the early afternoon, throw a *frozen* haunch on it, and go hunting. Upon your return, the fire will have burned out, and there will be your smoked venison, perfectly done. There are many variables to this method, however, such as the size fire you build, the size of the roast, and the temperature of the air. If you can work out a formula for predictable results, let us know. We don't mind experimenting, so we sometimes put the frozen meat in the smoker and go hunting for the rest of the day, but the results cannot be guaranteed (or even duplicated).

Do Look a Gift Haunch in the Mouth

Potato-Turnip Flan

SERVES 6

1 pound of white turnips (You will need 2 heaping cups of peeled, cubed turnips.)
1 large white potato, ⅔ cup cubed
3 tablespoons butter
2 large eggs
½ cup milk
3 tablespoons heavy cream
½ teaspoon freshly grated nutmeg
½ teaspoon salt
Chopped parsley for garnish

This is a delicately flavored custard with a nice texture. It's not the usual slippery custard because the puréed turnip retains some fiber and the potatoes are put through a sieve or food mill and contribute denseness to the mixture. It is a perfect accompaniment to venison or roast beef.

Preheat oven to 375°.

Peel and roughly chop the turnips and place them in a heavy-bottomed saucepan with a cover. Add a small amount of water, bring to a boil, and simmer approximately 20 minutes, or until tender. Peel, roughly chop, and boil the potato in another pan.

Remove the turnips from the heat, drain, then purée them in a food processor or food mill. Add the butter and remaining ingredients, except the potato, and process another 10 seconds.

Push the potato through a sieve with a wooden spoon and add to the turnip mixture. It is very important to flavor and texture to cook the potato separately and not to purée it. Do not take a shortcut with this step.

Pour the mixture into a 9-inch buttered cake pan or quiche pan. Set inside a roasting pan and pour hot water to a level at least halfway up the outside of the cake or quiche pan. Place in the preheated oven and cook for 30 minutes. When the custard is set, a knife inserted into it will come out clean.

Garnish around the edges with chopped parsley. Serve warm, although this recipe is good tepid or even cold.

Spinach Soufflé in Tomato Halves

SERVES 6 TO 8

Preheat oven to 375°.

Cut the tops off the tomatoes and, using a grapefruit knife, cut the centers out. Slice a tiny bit off the bottom of any tomato that does not stand up straight. Sprinkle the insides with salt and turn upside down on a paper towel to drain for 20 minutes. Meanwhile, cook the spinach just until wilted in a small amount of water. Drain in a colander and press with a wooden spoon to extract as much liquid as possible. Squeeze it with your hands when it is cool enough.

Melt the butter in a frying pan with the oil. Press the garlic and add it to the pan, stirring for one minute. Add the spinach and sauté for 5 minutes to evaporate all the liquid.

Remove the spinach from the heat and purée it in a food processor or food mill, then add the egg yolks and 4 tablespoons of the cheese. Add salt and pepper to taste.

Beat the egg whites until stiff and fold them into the spinach mixture. Fill the tomatoes with the spinach mixture and sprinkle the remaining 2 tablespoons of cheese over the top of the filled tomatoes. Bake in a shallow pan, uncovered, for 20 minutes. Serve immediately.

This is not only a delicious way to serve two great vegetables, but it also lends eye appeal to the buffet or place setting with its colorful appearance.

1 medium-size tomato per person
2 pounds fresh spinach, well washed with stems removed, or 2 packages frozen leaf spinach
4 eggs, separated
2 teaspoons garlic put through a garlic press
6 tablespoons Parmesan cheese, freshly grated
Salt and pepper to taste
2 tablespoons butter
2 tablespoons oil

Hearts of Palm Salad

SERVES 8

1/3 cup salad oil
2 tablespoons lemon juice
1 teaspoon sugar
1/2 teaspoon salt
1/2 teaspoon angostura bitters
1/4 teaspoon paprika
2 tablespoons finely chopped
   stuffed olives
1 tablespoon finely chopped
   onion
1 tablespoon finely chopped
   celery
One 14-ounce can hearts of
   palm, drained and sliced
4 cups torn Bibb lettuce (6 to 8
   heads, depending on size)

Combine salad oil, lemon juice, sugar, salt, bitters, paprika, olives, onion, and celery. Whisk well and chill. At serving time, toss together the hearts of palm and lettuce. Add dressing, toss lightly, and serve immediately.

Applesauce Tarts

SERVES 8

8 slices of very thin white
   bread
8 tablespoons softened butter
2½ cups homemade applesauce

This is a very easy and tasty dessert, especially if you have made extra Spiced Applesauce (*which see*). It is more elegant looking than apple crisp, but it has the same suggestion of autumn in its flavor.

Preheat oven to 350°.

Remove crusts and butter the bread on one side. Cut off a small triangle from each corner of each slice and reserve. Press the bread slices gently into a muffin tin, buttered side down, to create a shell. Fill the bread cups with applesauce, dot with butter, and put two reserved bread triangles, butter side up, on top of each tart to create a lid. Bake for 30 minutes.

Cool for 5 minutes and remove each tart from the muffin tin with a knife tip, and place on individual serving plates. Serve warm or at room temperature with whipped cream or softened vanilla ice cream on top, if desired.

THREE

IKE EISENHOWER'S FAVORITE HUNT LUNCHEON

January

QUAIL HASH ON BUTTERED WILD RICE

◆

BOSTON AND BIBB LETTUCE SALAD WITH
TRUE FRENCH DRESSING

◆

BUTTERMILK CORN BREAD STICKS

◆

MAYHAW JELLY OR WINE JELLY

◆

PERSIMMON ICE CREAM

◆

ALMOND-CHOCOLATE LACE COOKIES

When George Humphrey was President Eisenhower's Secretary of the Treasury, he frequently entertained Ike and Mamie at his Milestone Plantation in Thomasville, Georgia. He was a neighbor and close friend of my husband's parents, Kathryn and Ralph Perkins, whose Springhill Plantation was right up the road from Milestone.

In the late forties and fifties, Springhill Plantation had more wild turkey than it did quail and wild turkey drives were often staged there. The guns would be ranged along a road or clearing, and at daybreak the turkeys would be driven from their roosts high in the pines, soaring out at treetop level. There might be as many as thirty or forty turkeys rocketing overhead, looking for all the world like a fleet of B-52 bombers, and just about as invulnerable to a shotgun. (Turkeys must be hit in the head to be stopped. Their heavy feathers are like an armor plate and even if a wing is broken they will hit the ground running and then outrun a horse. They're so fast on the takeoff that one rarely gets a second shot.)

In short, this was exciting shooting in anyone's book, and when conditions were right, invitations would be issued in code by telephone the evening before the drive. In those days, everyone had a party line and it would not do to inform the whole neighborhood (including all the poachers) where the turkeys were roosting. No matter what the plans were for the morrow, everyone invited immediately accepted the invitation and scrapped other engagements.

Thus it was that Dwight Eisenhower would be invited to shoot wild turkeys on Springhill Plantation. He would frequently stay on to hunt quail and have luncheon afterward. He declared this recipe to be his favorite way of preparing quail and he always demanded (and got) Quail Hash as it was made by Mrs. Perkins's cook, Jessie Hill.

This recipe can be used with California quail, pheasant, or chicken.

Quail Hash on Buttered Wild Rice

SERVES 6

Put the quail in a heavy saucepan. Add 2 cups of water, the onion, and the celery. Cover and simmer gently for 15 minutes. Remove the quail and set aside to cool. Reserve poaching liquid, discard onion and celery, and boil to reduce liquid to 1 cup. Add the light cream or milk and set aside.

Bone the cooled quail and cut into julienne strips. Set aside.

Start preparing the wild rice. It will need to boil 45 minutes. Put the rice in a large saucepan and add 4 or 5 cups of water. Bring to a boil, then lower the heat and simmer for 15 minutes. Strain the dark brown water off, rinse the rice, and start all over—replace the rice in the pan, add 4 or 5 cups of fresh water and boil another 15 minutes. Repeat the process once more: strain, add fresh water and return to the boil a 3rd time. About 10 minutes into the 3rd period, or after 40 minutes of cooking, watch the rice to see if the jackets of each grain have burst. If they have, the rice is done. It should not be overcooked to a mushy consistency— this would ruin the flavor and texture. Wild rice should be chewy in texture and nutty in flavor.

Drain the last time, and leave the rice in the sieve over some simmering water to keep warm while you prepare the sauce.

12 quail, cleaned, plucked, and ready to cook
1 medium onion, roughly sliced
5 stalks celery, roughly cut
½ cup light cream or whole milk (depending on your attitude toward calories)
1½ cups uncooked wild rice

Sauce

3 tablespoons butter

3 tablespoons potato or rice flour (This is finer and won't lump as readily as regular flour. It is available in most markets. Swan brand is manufactured by Citrus Corporation of America, Chicago, Illinois 60606.)

1½ cups liquid (1 cup reduced poaching liquid plus ½ cup light cream or milk, heated)

4 medium shallots, finely minced

1 celery stalk, finely minced

¼ cup fresh parsley, minced

1 teaspoon chervil

1 teaspoon salt

Freshly ground pepper to taste

½ teaspoon freshly ground nutmeg

While the rice is boiling, melt 3 tablespoons of butter in a heavy saucepan. Add 3 tablespoons potato or rice flour and let bubble gently for 3 minutes over medium heat to cook the flour. Heat the poaching mixture liquid and pour it into the flour and butter, whisking constantly until thick and creamy. Set aside over hot (not boiling) water in a double boiler.

Sauté the parsley, shallots, and celery over low to medium heat until soft, but not browned. Add to the sauce in the double boiler with the chervil, and salt and pepper to taste. Grate the nutmeg into the sauce and add the julienned quail. Mix thoroughly. Heat just long enough to warm the quail and serve over the boiled and buttered wild rice.

The secret is not to overcook the quail while poaching it, and not to leave it in the heated sauce too long before serving, as this will result in tough quail.

Boston and Bibb Lettuce Salad

SERVES 6 TO 8

2 heads Boston lettuce

6 small heads Bibb lettuce

Wash and dry the greens and refrigerate in plastic bags. When ready to serve, arrange in a salad bowl or on individual plates, sparingly pour True French dressing over all, and toss lightly.

True French Dressing

⅓ cup raspberry vinegar

1 cup extra virgin olive oil

1 teaspoon Dijon mustard

1 teaspoon balsamic vinegar

2 large cloves of garlic, put through a garlic press

¼ teaspoon salt

Freshly ground pepper to taste

To avoid heartburn, slice peeled cloves of garlic in half lengthwise and remove and discard any trace of the green shoot inside. Press the garlic into a large bowl. Add the other ingredients except oil, and whisk. Pour the oil in slowly while whisking vigorously. Pour sparingly over greens and toss lightly.

Buttermilk Corn Bread

SERVES ABOUT 12

Spread a heavy iron skillet (8 or 9 inch) or cornstick molds with bacon drippings, and put in a very hot oven (450°) to heat. Mix together the cornmeal, salt, soda, and baking powder.

Add the buttermilk and bacon drippings. Mix well and pour into the heated pan or molds. Bake 20 minutes at 400°, or until well browned.

I don't usually advocate using packaged mixes, but

*2 cups white or yellow
  cornmeal*
1 teaspoon salt
½ teaspoon baking soda
1 teaspoon baking powder
1¼ cups buttermilk
*2 tablespoons melted bacon
  drippings*

it is hard to improve on the cornmeal-muffin mixes available. If you are short of time use one, but grease the pan or molds with bacon drippings to give it that homemade flavor.

Mayhaw jelly is the ideal accompaniment for quail. It is invariably served with biscuits or cornbread when quail is on the menu. The only trouble is that it is hard to find. The sole reason I mention it is to alert you to the name and tell you that if you ever see any while traveling in the South, buy it all. Even Southern cooks have trouble finding the elusive Mayhaw. The closest thing to it is this sherry wine jelly made with the particular sherry mentioned.

Wine Jelly

MAKES 4½ PINTS

4 envelopes unflavored gelatin
3½ cups sugar
Thin-sliced peel of 3 lemons
Juice of 3 lemons
3 cups Tio Pepe very dry sherry
½ cup light rum

This recipe can be served as a dessert with a thin zest of lemon peel to garnish it. It's good on toast or English muffins. It is a nourishing and delicious dish for invalids. It will go fast, but the recipe can be cut in half if you don't think you can use this much.

Put the gelatin in a large bowl and add ½ cup cold water to soften it. Add 3½ cups boiling water and 3½ cups sugar. Stir until the sugar and gelatin are dissolved. Add the lemon juice and rind, mix well, and add the sherry and rum.

Pour into jars and refrigerate at least 5 hours before serving.

Persimmon Ice Cream

The persimmons should be so soft that they feel like jelly inside their skins. If they are not ripe enough, you will pucker up your mouth at the first bite; the alum taste is unmistakable. A way to hasten the ripening process is to put the persimmons into the freezer overnight. Remove them when they are hard as baseballs and put them in a warm place to thaw. Just to make sure, taste a tiny bit of the fruit before starting this recipe. If they still taste of alum, let them stand in a warm place for another day or so and try again. If the persimmons are ripe enough, the stems will pull out with the white membrane attached to them.

Cut the fruit in half. Some don't have seeds, some do. Remove them if they do. Remove any blemishes or price stickers from the skin. Place them all in a food processor or blender and purée, then set aside. If you have any purée left over, freeze it and use it later to make Persimmon Pudding (*which see*).

Combine milk, sugar, and eggs in a heavy pan and put over medium heat. Cook, stirring constantly, until thick. Remove from heat, add vanilla, and cool. Fold in the persimmon purée and freeze according to the directions on your ice cream machine. If you don't have an ice cream maker, freeze in ice cube trays until set, remove to a large bowl, beat for 3 minutes, then return to the freezing unit of your refrigerator until ready to serve.

2 cups persimmon purée (5 to 6 medium persimmons, very ripe)
3 cups milk
1 cup sugar
1 teaspoon vanilla extract
6 eggs

Almond-Chocolate Lace Cookies

MAKES ABOUT 20 COOKIES

½ cup (1 stick) butter

½ cup sugar

1 tablespoon all-purpose flour

¼ teaspoon salt

¾ cup ground blanched
   almonds

2 tablespoons milk

1 teaspoon almond extract

3½ ounces semisweet
   chocolate, melted in a 200°
   oven

It is best to serve these cookies within 1 hour of baking, or else freeze them and serve them right out of the freezer.

Preheat oven to 200°.

Place chocolate in a tempered glass bowl and put it in the oven for about 10 minutes. Use semisweet bits (they will melt more quickly), or cut chocolate squares into rather small pieces.

Line 2 cookie sheets with foil and butter and flour them, shaking excess flour off. Melt the ½ cup butter in a skillet over medium heat. Add the sugar, flour, and salt, and stir until the sugar dissolves, about 3 minutes. Mix in the almonds and milk and stir until slightly thickened. Remove from the heat and blend in the almond extract.

Remove the chocolate from the oven and set it aside in a warm place. Reset the oven temperature to 350°.

Drop the batter onto the prepared baking sheets by teaspoons, spacing them 3½ to 4 inches apart. Bake the cookies, one sheet at a time, until light golden brown, about 5 to 7 minutes. Let stand 2 minutes to firm, then remove and transfer to a wire rack or waxed paper to cool.

Using a thin, flexible knife or spatula, spread a layer of the melted chocolate on the bottom side of a cookie. Cover with the flat side of another cookie to make a sandwich. Cool until the chocolate is set. Serve within 1 hour or wrap in plastic wrap and put into the freezer. Serve these right out of the freezer directly to the table—they will be crisp and absolutely delicious. They keep in the freezer up to 6 months, so you can make them well in advance of any presidential visit.

FOUR

IN MEMORY OF THE TAKARO CLUB

February

STUFFED ROASTED LEG OF LAMB

◆

MUSHROOM CUSTARD

◆

TOMATO AND BASIL SALAD

◆

ROBERT MONDAVI NAPA VALLEY CABERNET SAUVIGNON

◆

HAZELNUT TORTE

New Zealand is so beautiful and the dry-fly fishing is so challenging that every serious angler should go there once. It is also very firm in its determination to be a thoroughly middle-class country. It has been called "Super Suburbia of the Southern Seas" and "The Gourmet's Purgat'ry"*

There was a first-class lodge there for about two or three years. It was called the Takaro Club, and it was on the South Island near Te Anu. One could drive to it if one had an extra week, but the best way to get there was via charter plane from Christchurch. The flight over the snow-capped Remarkable Mountains in a single-engine plane immediately following a thirty-hour flight from New York was noteworthy in itself. Equally stimulating was the announcement by the pilot after an hour and a half: "We *should* be right over it now, but I don't see anything down there . . . Hah! There's a grassy strip right along the river. OK, we're going in."

A perfect landing was completed, and one look at the clubhouse and outbuildings explained it all. Two feet of tall grass blew in the wind on every sod roof in the entire complex. Architecturally, the place was a show-stopper. Heavy beam construction using the local red cedar held up the weighty earth and grass overhead. Glass from floor to ceiling gave onto spectacular mountain views on every side. A California owner and a California architect had created a memorable group of buildings.

A choice collection of New Zealand paintings hung on the walls. The billiard room was a classic Edwardian retreat. There was a swimming pool and a sauna. Every suite consisted of a paneled sitting room with fireplace, bedroom, bath, and a terrace overlooking the White-stone River.

The guides were knowledgeable fly fishermen. The chef was Austrian and turned out dainties such as Quail Eggs in Aspic and Hazelnut Torte. The lights would go up in the dining room when he rolled in the entrée on a mahogany cart. The wine cellar was exceedingly good, and there was even a Takaro Club tie. Wow! After thirty-six hours without sleep, it looked like a dream. And apparently it was.

Alas, the government decided it didn't want an

---

* Wynford Vaughan-Thomas; in (you guessed it) *Farewell to New Zealand.*

American to own five thousand acres in New Zealand, and there went the most elegant fishing lodge in the Southern Hemisphere. One wonders what ever became of that splendid group of buildings. Is it a retirement home for senile socialists, or is it abandoned, just growing more grass on the roofs?

Now we stay in a nice, clean, dull motel right in town and cook in the tiny kitchenette. No one dims or brightens the lights when dinner is served, and no one thinks of a necktie. After all, one is outdoors at least twelve hours every day, and who needs luxurious surroundings and exquisite service after twelve hours of fishing in the rain?

What follows is a simplified version of a dinner at the Takaro Club.

Stuffed Roasted Leg of Lamb

SERVES 8 TO 10

Preheat oven to 450°.

Boil the rice in salted water for 20 minutes. Drain and place the rice in a sieve over simmering water to steam for an additional 20 to 25 minutes, until it is tender and dry.

Cook the spinach, squeeze out the excess water (you can wrap the spinach in a dish towel to do this, if you wish), and chop.

Melt the ¼ pound of butter and the oil in a heavy-bottomed skillet and sauté the chopped onion, garlic, and mint for 10 minutes, stirring occasionally. Do not brown.

Add the chopped ham and spinach to the skillet and mix well. Remove from the heat and add the bread crumbs, egg, and salt and pepper to taste. Mix well.

Spread the butterflied lamb open, salt and pepper the inside surfaces, and spread the bread-crumb-spinach mixture on top. Add the rice over all and bring up the sides of the lamb to enclose the stuffing. Hold the meat

A 7- to 8-pound leg of lamb or shoulder, boned and butterflied (4 to 5 pounds boned)
½ cup long grain rice
½ cup cooked minced ham
½ cup onion, finely chopped
1 cup cooked, chopped spinach
1½ cups fresh bread crumbs
1 egg
2 cloves garlic, put through a garlic press
4 tablespoons fresh chopped mint, or 1½ tablespoons dried mint
2 tablespoons oil
¼ pound butter, plus 2 tablespoons butter to rub on lamb
1 tablespoon flour to rub on lamb
1 bouquet garni, composed of 6 sprigs parsley, 2 bay leaves, and 2 sprigs thyme, tied together with a string
Salt and freshly ground pepper to taste
1 tablespoon rosemary

in place with a skewer while you tie up the ends. Truss it in several places also, so that it resembles a nice, square parcel.

Rub the outside of the roast with butter and flour and place it in an open roasting pan on top of the *bouquet garni*. Sprinkle the top with the 1 tablespoon rosemary. Place in the preheated oven for 30 minutes. Then reduce the heat to 325° and cook for 45 minutes longer.

Remove from the oven and allow to stand for at least 15 minutes before carving. It will continue to cook even after you have removed it from the oven. The internal temperature should be 130° to 150°, depending upon whether you like your lamb pink in the center or brown. You've spent a bundle for this meat; don't overcook it to dry tastelessness.

Since this recipe is a complete meal in itself with the rice and spinach stuffing, a light and savory accompaniment to complement the delicious lamb flavor is all that is needed to complete the dish. The following recipe for Mushroom Custard not only fills the bill, but could also be used for luncheon with a salad, or for a brunch.

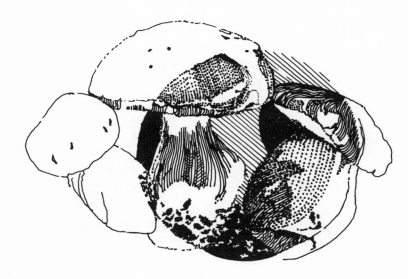

Mushroom Custard

This must be prepared the night before cooking and serving.

Melt the butter and oil in a large skillet over medium heat. Sauté the onions, celery, and green pepper for 7 to 8 minutes. Add the sliced mushrooms and sauté until all vegetables are soft but not brown. Sprinkle with salt and pepper, then remove from the heat and let cool. Stir in the mayonnaise. Spread the crustless bread with the soft butter, and cut each into ½-inch cubes. Place half the bread cubes in a lightly buttered 13 × 9 × 2-inch baking dish.

Pour the sautéed vegetable mixture over the top. Add the remaining bread cubes. Beat the eggs with the milk and pour over the casserole.

Cover with foil and refrigerate overnight. The next day, preheat the oven to 325°, and bake 45 minutes, uncovered. Remove from the oven and sprinkle sharp grated cheddar evenly over the top. Return to the oven and bake 15 minutes longer.

That this recipe must be started the night before serving is a plus for the harried host or hostess, who can slide it into the oven and join the guests for 45 minutes without worrying. After wrestling with that leg of lamb all morning, one deserves a break.

1¼ pounds fresh mushrooms, sliced
3 tablespoons butter
2 tablespoons oil
½ cup onions, chopped finely
½ cup celery, chopped finely
½ cup green bell pepper, chopped finely
½ teaspoon each of salt and freshly ground black pepper
½ cup mayonnaise
6 slices bread, with crusts removed
2 tablespoons soft butter
2 eggs, beaten
1½ cups milk
1 cup shredded cheddar cheese

Tomato and Basil Salad

SERVES 8

4 large ripe tomatoes
1 cup fresh basil leaves,
    chopped
Salt and freshly ground black
    pepper to taste
⅓ cup rosé wine
⅔ cup extra virgin olive oil

Slice the tomatoes, allowing ½ tomato for each serving. Arrange slices on individual salad plates. Sprinkle the roughly chopped basil on top, and add salt and freshly ground pepper to taste.

Whisk the oil into the wine and spoon sparingly over the tomatoes and basil. This salad is very good when the tomatoes are right out of the garden along with the fresh basil. Even hothouse tomatoes are edible with basil sprinkled over them. Basil can be grown all year long in a sunny window, so get some seeds and plant 3 or 4 pots of it right now so you'll have it available.

The dressing is one you will use every time you want to serve wine through a salad course. There is no vinegar or lemon juice to fight with the noble vintage you are pouring. Of course, you can serve the salad following the entrée, as is usual, but if you are serving a buffet meal where everything goes on one plate and are serving a wine with it, this is the perfect solution: a salad dressing with no acid bite.

Hazelnut Torte

SERVES 8 TO 12

¾ cup hazelnuts
Eight 1-ounce squares
    unsweetened chocolate
½ pound unsalted butter,
    softened at room temperature
    for 1 hour
1 cup sugar
6 egg whites
Pinch of salt
2 tablespoons butter (for pan)
2 tablespoons all-purpose flour
    (for pan)

CAKE

Preheat oven to 200°.

Warm the hazelnuts in the preheated oven for 15 minutes. Replace them in the oven with the unsweetened chocolate, in a tempered glass dish. While the nuts are still hot, rub them in a clean terry-cloth hand towel to remove the skins. Grind the nuts in a blender or food processor until they are as fine as flour. This *is* the flour!

Remove the melted chocolate from the oven and

increase the temperature to 375°. Set the chocolate aside to cool.

Beat the butter with the sugar until creamy, then add the chocolate and the nut flour. Mix well.

Whip the egg whites with the pinch of salt until very stiff, fold a small amount of the whites into the chocolate mixture to lighten it, and then pour the chocolate mixture over the egg whites and fold in carefully.

Thoroughly butter a midsize, very shallow roasting pan, place a sheet of parchment paper in the bottom and butter and flour it. Or, use 3 round layer-cake pans, thoroughly buttered and floured. Pour the batter into the pan or divide evenly among the 3 layer pans and bake in the preheated oven for 12 to 15 minutes.

FILLING

While the cake is baking, prepare the filling. Cook the sugar with the coffee until it is syrupy, about 3 or 4 minutes. Let it cool.

½ cup sugar
¼ cup very strong espresso coffee
4 squares semisweet chocolate, softened
⅓ pound butter
6 egg yolks
½ pint whipping cream
2 tablespoons confectioner's sugar

Mix in the softened chocolate and butter. Add the egg yolks 1 at a time while constantly stirring. The filling should thicken as the eggs are beaten in. Cool before using.

Cut the torte (if you have baked it in 1 pan) into 3 pieces, lengthwise. Now you will have either a long rectangular torte or a round torte. (The disagreement about whether torten should be round or rectangular is still going on in Vienna.) Fill between each layer with the chocolate filling, and spread the remainder on the sides and top. Whip the cream and the sugar and decorate around the bottom and top edges with a pastry tube using a star tip, and, if you like, place some candied violets or candied rose petals on top to make it look completely Viennese. Chill in the refrigerator for at least 1 hour before serving.

Even though there isn't an Austrian chef left in Te Anu, there is still the nearby dry-fly fishing, which can be superb, and there are some delightful sheep dogs (and millions of sheep) around.

I will never forget my enchantment at seeing a shepherd on a motorcycle roaring down the road with his three sheepdogs in the sidecar. If you can get a shepherd to demonstrate what a strong-eyed sheepdog can do, then by all means delay the fishing for fifteen minutes while an intense, efficient Border Collie does his stuff.

Dunedin and many of the small towns nearby are almost entirely Scottish, and while driving to a stream in the area we entered a little town named Waipahi Junction and were astounded by the sight of thirty-five kiltie bands with bagpipes skirling and drums pounding. We pulled over and watched the best parade we've ever seen.

You can drive south of Invercargill and look out to sea at Steward Island, the last landfall north of Antarctica. The scenery is gorgeous, and I understand that some new lodges are being built. We can't wait to go back.

FIVE

WHERE ARE YOU GOING? CXI VIA VK, OF COURSE.

February

OCTOPUS IN CURRY SAUCE (KIKA IN GILBERTESE)

◆

JAPANESE BEER

◆

PURÉE OF VEGETABLES KIRIBATI

◆

CABBAGE SALAD WITH BOILED DRESSING

◆

MANGO MOUSSE

Here's a little quiz for the jet-set fly fishers out there. The luggage tags read CXI for your final destination. The code letters for your airline are VK. Don't rush for your OAG, it's not in there. I'll give you another clue or two.

Captain James Cook discovered this place on December 24, 1777. One of the small offshore islands bears his name. A French Jesuit priest later settled there and named the area in which he lived Paris. Across the channel lies (of course) London. South and west of Paris one will find Poland. During World War II the U.S. built a runway to the northeast that can handle anything that flies. Near the airport is the serene little village of Banana.

This could be only one place in the world. Yes, you've got it: It is Christmas Island, CXI, naturally. It is truly superb frontier-fly-fishing territory. The fishing areas have less romantic names than the town. Two of the best are "M-site" and "Y-site," so named when the U.K. and the U.S. were conducting atomic bomb tests between 1954 and 1965. There is still evidence of their activity out in the bush in the form of abandoned equipment.

The Captain Cook Hotel is a former officer's quarters built of cement block with a tin roof. There is a nice lanai overlooking the beach. It has a thatched roof and a constantly refreshing breeze (or gale) blowing through it. It's a perfect place to have a drink before or after dinner. Once a week the hotel puts on a delicious steak and lobster grill overlooking the crashing surf. The octopus are gathered up right out in front on the coral flats at low tide, by two ladies. One has a stick with a hook on the end of it. She pries the small octopi out of the coral rock. The other woman holds a burlap bag into which the writhing creatures are dropped. In an hour and a half they have enough to feed about sixty people. If you haven't tried octopus or squid, this is an easy way to begin. Squid should either be prepared very quickly over high heat (cooked no more than three minutes), as they do in Greece, or stewed for not less than half an hour, as they are done in this recipe. Like game birds, they toughen quickly when cooked. Unfortunately, it is a state of toughness that has most often been encountered by many first-(and last-) time eaters.

Christmas Island is thirteen hundred miles south of Honolulu in the Line Islands. Together with the Phoenix and Gilbert Islands it makes up the Republic of Kiribati (pronounced Keer-ah-bahs). There are thirty-three islands scattered over a mind-boggling twenty-two million square miles of the Pacific. Obviously, most foodstuffs have to be taken in by air. The only thing that grows in abundance is the coconut palm. This recipe uses ingredients that typically would be flown in, plus the everpresent coconut.

Octopus in Curry Sauce (Kika)

SERVES 6

3 medium-sized white potatoes,
  cubed
4 tablespoons butter
2 tablespoons oil
1 teaspoon curry powder
6 carrots, shredded
½ cup coconut milk
2 medium-sized onions,
  shredded
4 stalks celery, finely minced
2 pounds small octopus or
  squid
Salt and freshly ground black
  pepper to taste

Have your fish market prepare the octopus for cooking, or, if you have caught them yourself, see the Appendix. They can be purchased frozen.

Place the octopus or squid in a large saucepan, cover with water, and boil for 30 minutes. Drain the water off and cut the octopus, including tentacles, into small cubes. Melt the butter and oil in a large frying pan and sauté the octopus and vegetables for 30 minutes, stirring frequently and adding more butter if necessary.

Add the coconut milk and the curry powder, salt and pepper to taste, mix well, cover, and cook for an additional hour, or until the octopus is tender.

You can serve this on a bed of fluffy white rice, or just serve it plain, as they do on Christmas Island. It's delicious, and it's a pretty good bet that you will be the first on your block to serve it.

Purée of Vegetables Kiribati

SERVES 6

3 tablespoons bacon fat
1 large yellow onion, chopped
1 large garlic clove, put through
  a garlic press
½ medium-sized green pepper,
  cored, seeded, and shredded
4 tablespoons coconut,
  shredded (fresh if possible)
One 10-ounce package frozen
  chopped spinach, or 1 cup
  cooked fresh spinach, drained
Half of a 10-ounce package
  frozen cut okra, or 15
  medium-sized fresh okra
  pods, cut into rounds

Preheat oven to 325°.

In a large frying pan melt the bacon fat over medium-high heat. Add the onion, garlic, green pepper, spinach, okra, and both potatoes. If you don't have a shredder or a food processor, dice all the vegetables to a fairly small size so they will cook quickly. Sauté them, stirring occasionally until they are limp and easily mashed with a fork, about 20 minutes.

Then add the shredded coconut, chives, thyme, nutmeg, salt and pepper to taste. Mix thoroughly and cook about 5 minutes more.

Cool slightly, and then purée in batches in a food processor or a food mill. Place in a buttered 4-cup soufflé dish or other deep ovenproof bowl.

Sauté the shredded carrot in 1 tablespoon butter in

a small frying pan and place it on top of the spinach mixture in a decorative pattern for garnish.

This recipe can be made ahead up to this point and refrigerated with a cover of foil or plastic wrap until you want to use it. Twenty minutes before serving, put the dish in a preheated oven with the foil cover and heat through. If it has thickened and become stiff, stir in 1 or 2 tablespoons of cream before serving it. This recipe goes well with fish or seafood. It has a delicate flavor and a slightly granular texture. Most people will know there is spinach in it, but they'll never guess the rest of the ingredients.

1 large Idaho potato, peeled and shredded
1 medium-sized sweet potato or yam, peeled and shredded
1 tablespoon minced fresh chives
¼ teaspoon crumbled leaf thyme
¼ teaspoon freshly grated nutmeg
1 teaspoon salt
Freshly ground pepper to taste
1 shredded carrot for garnish
1 tablespoon butter

Cabbage Salad with Boiled Dressing

SERVES 6

Put everything except the vinegar and the cabbage in the top of a double boiler over barely simmering, not boiling, water. Mix well. Add the vinegar gradually, whisking constantly until thickened. Cool, pour over shredded cabbage, toss well, and chill before serving.

1 medium-sized head of cabbage, shredded
1 scant teaspoon salt
1 teaspoon dry mustard
1½ tablespoons granulated sugar
1 grind of cayenne pepper
2 tablespoons potato or rice flour
1 whole egg, slightly beaten
1½ tablespoons melted butter
¾ cup milk
¼ cup tarragon vinegar

Mango Mousse

2 cups fresh ripe mango pulp, or
½ pound dried mangoes
reconstituted overnight by
soaking in water
⅓ cup sugar or equivalent
amount of sugar substitute
¾ cup half-and-half
½ cup sour cream or plain
yogurt
⅓ cup fresh lemon or lime juice
(If you can get Key limes, it's
even better.)
1 teaspoon grated lemon or
lime peel
1 packet unflavored gelatin
2 tablespoons dry white wine
½ teaspoon freshly grated
nutmeg
Mint leaves for garnish

If using dried mangoes, drain the water off them in a sieve. If using fresh ones, see the recipe for Mango Sherbet for instructions on peeling and seeding.

Soften the gelatin in the wine in a small tempered glass cup. Set this in a pan of simmering water and stir until the gelatin is dissolved. Add the sugar or sugar substitute, lemon juice, and the gelatin mixture to the mangoes and purée them in a food processor or food mill. With the food processor running add the light cream, the sour cream or yogurt, the grated lemon peel, and the nutmeg through the feed tube and run a few seconds until well combined. If doing this by hand, add these ingredients to the mango purée in a bowl and whisk well.

Pour into a crystal or clear-glass serving bowl or individual footed dessert dishes. The color is so beautiful that it shouldn't be hidden. Chill 3 to 4 hours. Garnish with the mint leaves.

This menu is a fairly exotic one, but not so different as to put "diners of good health" (as M. F. K. Fisher phrases it) into a state of alarm. The chef at the Captain Cook Hotel on Christmas Island kindly furnished me with the recipe for Octopus in Curry Sauce. I ate two helpings of it and skipped the grilled steak.

By the way, if you do find yourself on Christmas Island in the near future, ask your guide to help you find a few Mantis Shrimp during a low tide. They are about the size of a 1½-pound Maine lobster. Take them to the hotel where the cook will prepare them for you. They are a rare treat.

Postscript: "VK" stands for Tungaru Airlines.

SIX

YES, VIRGINIA, THERE *ARE* SNIPE HUNTS

February

ROAST SNIPE SERVED ON TOAST POINTS WITH GIBLET PÂTÉ

◆

ONION TART WITH OLIVES AND ANCHOVIES

◆

BRAISED MATCHSTICK CARROTS

◆

JORDAN ALEXANDER VALLEY CABERNET SAUVIGNON

◆

GREEN SALAD WITH FRENCH DRESSING

◆

RASPBERRY SOUFFLÉ

Our best snipe hunts occur in northern Florida after the duck season is over and the big flooded cornfield (which is the main duck pond) is being drained. The snipe dart around the edges of the receding water and tower straight up when they are disturbed by the Labrador Retrievers. It's snappy shooting, and although we don't get great numbers of them, as they do in England, there are nevertheless enough for a dinner later in the week.

Snipe are very rich in spite of their small size. Two per person will normally suffice. When cleaning, be sure to save the giblets, including the trail or intestine. In only two birds, the woodcock and the snipe, are the intestines good to eat. They come in a tight little white coil and are always clean. The European tradition is to cook the birds without removing the innards, but it then becomes necessary to overcook the outer bird in order to cook the inner bird properly. It's much more palatable to prepare a small pâté from the giblets and serve it on toast under the roasted bird. In fact, it's downright delicious this way.

Roast Snipe

SERVES 6

12 snipe, oven ready
4 peeled shallots
6 sprigs fresh parsley
Grated rind of 1 lemon
2 tablespoons bread crumbs
Salt and pepper to taste
2 tablespoons red wine
2 tablespoons sour cream
2 tablespoons butter
6 slices thin white bread, toasted, buttered, and cut into 4 triangles

Preheat oven to 400°.

Place the snipe, breast up, in a shallow baking pan with a splash of water. Bake for 10 to 12 minutes. The internal temperature should be 140° to 150° when done.

Mince the shallots, parsley, and giblets together. Melt the butter in a small frying pan and sauté the mixture for 3 to 5 minutes, until the giblets are cooked. Add the bread crumbs, red wine, and grated lemon peel. Remove from the heat and add the sour cream and salt and pepper to taste. Spread the mixture generously on the toast points and place the birds on top. Serve at once.

Onion Tart with Olives and Anchovies

SERVES 6

PASTRY SHELL

Preheat oven to 375°.

Put the flour and salt in a food processor and run for 2 or 3 seconds to mix. Then drop in the butter, one pat at a time, processing until it is well incorporated into the flour, 8 to 10 seconds. While the machine is running, add the egg and water through the feed tube and allow to run a few seconds more until a ball of dough forms.

Remove dough from the processor bowl, roll out on a lightly floured surface, and place in a 9- or 10-inch pie pan, fluting the edges. Put into the freezer for 5 minutes.

You can also prepare this pastry by hand by cutting in the butter, then adding the egg and water and mixing lightly.

Bake in the preheated oven for 10 minutes. Remove and allow to cool. Meanwhile, reset the oven to 350° and begin to prepare the filling.

1½ cups flour
½ teaspoon salt
¼ pound butter, cut into 8 pieces
1 egg
3 tablespoons cold water

FILLING

Peel and slice the onions. (If you're doing it by hand, hold a quarter of a slice of bread in your mouth, and you won't cry.)

Melt the butter and oil in a large frying pan and add the onions. Cook over medium heat, turning frequently with a spatula. They will take about 20 to 25 minutes to turn a golden color. Do not brown.

Cut the olives in half lengthwise and pit them, if necessary. Drain the oil off the anchovies and place them on paper towels, patting them with another paper towel to remove excess oil. Set aside.

Grate the cheese in a food processor, add the cream cheese in chunks, and then the eggs, chervil, and pep-

10 to 12 medium-sized yellow onions
2 tablespoons butter
2 tablespoons oil
11 ounces cream cheese
½ teaspoon chervil
Freshly grated white pepper
½ pound Gruyère cheese, grated (1 heaping cup after grating)
3 eggs
One 2-ounce can anchovy fillets
12 Kalamata olives or ripe black olives, pitted

per. Run the machine just long enough to mix well.

If you don't have a food processor, grate the Gruyère by hand, and put it and the cream cheese in the frying pan, first removing the onions to a plate with a slotted spatula. Stir the cheeses until the cream cheese melts, add the chervil and pepper and mix well. Remove from the heat and add the slightly beaten eggs to the mixture, combining thoroughly.

To assemble, place the cooked onions in the pie shell, arrange the anchovies on top of them in a star-shaped pattern radiating from the center (so that each wedge will have some in it when cut). Space the olive halves evenly over the onions between the anchovy strips, and pour the cheese mixture over all. Bake in the pre-heated 350° oven for 20 minutes, or until the filling is set and golden brown on top. A knife inserted in the tart will come out clean when it is done.

Cool at least 15 minutes before cutting, or allow to cool 1 or 2 hours, and serve at room temperature.

If you happen to detest anchovies, leave them out. Do the same with the olives if you don't like them; you will be left with a delicious onion tart nevertheless.

Braised Matchstick Carrots

SERVES 6

8 parsley sprigs, chopped
12 carrots, medium size
3 tablespoons butter

Julienne the carrots to ⅛ inch in a food processor. If you have to do this by hand, make them as thin as possible.

Melt 1 tablespoon butter in a heavy-bottomed saucepan with a lid. Put the carrots in the pan, cover, and cook over very low heat for about 15 minutes, or until tender when pierced with a fork. Sprinkle the chopped parsley on top and serve at once.

For your salad use an assortment of greens and French Dressing (which see).

Raspberry Soufflé

SERVES 6

Preheat oven to 375°.

Prepare a 3-cup soufflé dish by buttering and then sugaring the bottom and sides. Put the frozen or slightly thawed raspberries in a food processor and purée them. If doing this by hand, thaw the berries completely and put through a food mill, or a sieve with a wooden spoon.

Beat the egg whites until stiff in a copper bowl and fold a small amount of them into the raspberry purée to lighten it. Then reverse the process and pour the purée into the egg whites and fold in carefully, but not necessarily completely—leave some egg white showing. Bake in the preheated oven for 20 minutes or until puffed and very slightly browned on top. Remove the soufflé dish from the oven, place it on a board or a heavy plate and take it to the table immediately.

The middle should still be soft when you serve it; a good soufflé always contains its own sauce, which is the center. Serve a firm outer piece, then spoon some of the soft center over each portion.

2 packages frozen sweetened raspberries
5 egg whites
1 teaspoon butter
1 teaspoon sugar

SEVEN

A SPECIAL PLANTATION DINNER

February

ROAST QUAIL ON GRIT CROUSTADINES

◆

PAIN DE LAITUES

◆

WILD RICE QUICHE

◆

BEAULIEU NAPA VALLEY CHAMPAGNE DE CHARDONNAY

◆

FROZEN CHOCOLATE MOUSSE

It doesn't matter how many times one walks up to a pointed covey of quail. The adrenalin is rushing, the heartbeat is up to attack level, the mouth is dry, the legs are rubbery, and WOW! there they go. Bang! . . . Bang! At least the rhythm of the two shots is right, even if the birds don't fall. One knows the seasoned southern quail hunter by the spaced shots. It should not be Bang Bang. Anyone who has walked in on enough covey points knows that there is always a sleeper. This is a quail that waits, hoping you will go away, but at the last minute loses his nerve and has to fly after all his buddies have flown. The novice blasts away at the first flush of birds and stands there with empty barrels, frantically trying to reload and shoot that last one who has waited to get up.

Then there is the really *smart* bird that waits until you are back in the shooting buggy with your gun unloaded and *then* takes off from under the wheels as you sit there like a dummy.

If you don't shoot your own wild quail, you can buy domestic quail that have been raised for the market. Or you can substitute Cornish game hens that you will find in almost any supermarket. The flavor of domestic birds will never be the same as that of wild, but they can be very satisfactory, nevertheless.

Roast Quail on Grit Croustadines

Birds should be at room temperature before roasting. Preheat the oven to 475°. Place the whole quail in a roasting pan, breast side up. Place half a slice of raw bacon on each breast so that the fat will baste the bird. Put a splash of water in the pan, but not enough to cover the bottom of the pan. Place the pan in the oven for 12 minutes. The internal temperature should be 140°. If you don't have a Thermicator, make a tiny slit along the breastbone and look at the meat. It should be light pink in the middle, shading to white on the outside. Salt and pepper to taste, place on a heated platter, breast side up, with a grit croustadine underneath each one. Garnish with big bunches of parsley or watercress at each end and serve. Allow 2 quail per person. If using the much larger Cornish game hens, one per person should be ample.

For the Grit Croustadines, use leftover grits from breakfast, or cook ½ cup quick grits, let them cool, then form them into patties. Or pour them into a clean tin soup can and chill in the refrigerator. Then slice into perfectly round patties and dredge them in flour and fry them in butter and a little oil until they are browned nicely. Place these under the quail on the heated platter to catch the juices. This is an old Southern way of serving this delectable little bird. A bit of the croustadine should be eaten along with every bite of quail.

If you have any leftover quail, bone them and make Quail Hash (*which see*). Do not parboil them; obviously they're already cooked. Use one cup of home-made chicken stock or canned chicken broth in place of the quail poaching liquid for your cream sauce.

A Special Plantation Dinner

Pain de Laitues

4 heads Boston lettuce (Do not try iceberg or leaf lettuce, they will not work; the lettuce must be very soft.)

3 tablespoons crème fraîche (Half heavy cream and half commercial sour cream. Mix together and let stand at room temperature while you are preparing the rest of the recipe.)

5 shallots, minced

½ cup minced ham

1 teaspoon allspice

3 eggs

½ cup milk

4 thin slices white bread with crusts removed, cubed

1 teaspoon salt

¼ teaspoon pepper, freshly ground

Preheat oven to 350°.

Prepare 8 tempered glass pottery custard cups by buttering them. Cut small rounds of aluminum foil to place in the bottom of each cup. Grease the foil once you have put it in place. This may seem like a big fuss, but they will unmold perfectly every time.

Put 2 cups of water into a large soup kettle and bring to a boil. Drop the washed lettuce into the boiling water, lower the heat, and simmer for 10 minutes. Pour the lettuce out of the kettle into a colander and run cold water over it. Let it drain well and squeeze it with your hands or in a towel to remove *all* water. Chop finely, and place in a large mixing bowl.

Soak the cubed bread in the milk while you mince the shallots and ham. Put all the ingredients into the bowl with the lettuce and mix thoroughly. Fill the custard cups ¾ full and place them in a shallow baking pan. Pour boiling water into the baking pan so that it comes at least halfway up the sides of the custard cups. Place the pan in the preheated oven for 30 to 40 minutes. They will be puffed and slightly browned when done. Unmold onto a warm platter, remove the foil inserts with the tip of a knife and garnish with big bunches of parsley at either end of the platter.

This vegetable goes perfectly with chicken, pheasant, or any white-meat bird. It can also be baked and served in one large casserole or soufflé dish in a bain-marie. Increase the cooking time by approximately 10 minutes. It will hold well in a warm oven for half an hour, perhaps deflating a tiny bit, but essentially unharmed.

Wild Rice Quiche

SERVES 6 TO 8

SHELL

Make an unbaked pie shell, as for Onion Tart (*which see*). Mix one egg yolk, a splash of water, and ½ teaspoon salt. Brush this egg mixture over the shell, prick in several places with a fork, and bake the shell for 10 minutes at 375°. Remove from the oven and set aside.

FILLING

Heat the oil in a large frying pan over medium heat and sauté the garlic. Do not let it brown, just cook it to the soft stage. Add the well-drained tomatoes, rice, cream cheese, and salt and pepper.

Stir over low heat until the cream cheese melts. Mix a small amount of the rice mixture into the beaten eggs and then pour the eggs into the rice mixture and blend well. Pour into the crust and bake at 375° for 30 minutes. Let stand for 10 or 15 minutes before cutting. This quiche goes well with any game bird or chicken. It's suitable for a picnic because it tastes just as good at room temperature as it does warm.

1½ cups cooked wild rice (a generous ⅓ cup uncooked)
1 cup fresh or canned plum tomatoes, peeled and well drained
One 3-ounce package cream cheese
1 teaspoon salt
¼ teaspoon freshly ground pepper
4 eggs, lightly beaten
2 tablespoons cooking oil
2 cloves garlic, put through a garlic press

Frozen Chocolate Mousse

1 pound of semisweet chocolate
  (Dutch, if you can get it)
¾ cup heavy cream, whipped
3 egg whites beaten until stiff
  with 3 tablespoons sugar
3 tablespoons strong coffee
3 tablespoons cognac
2 egg yolks

FOR GARNISH:
½ pint heavy cream, whipped
2 tablespoons confectioner's
  sugar
1 teaspoon vanilla

Prepare a 4-cup soufflé dish by attaching a paper collar to the outside of the dish with a rubber band. It should extend above the rim of the dish by at least 3 inches.

Melt the chocolate in a tempered glass or metal container in a 200° oven. Remove the chocolate from the heat, place in a large bowl, and beat the egg yolks into it. Add the liqueur and the coffee. Mix well. Beat the whipping cream until stiff and fold into the chocolate mixture.

Beat the egg whites until stiff and add them to the chocolate mixture, first folding a small amount of the whites into the chocolate to lighten it, and then pouring the entire chocolate mixture into the whites. Fold carefully and pour into the prepared soufflé dish and freeze for at least 3 hours. Remove the paper collar when the mousse is set and decorate the top and bottom edges with whipped cream piped through a pastry bag with a star tip, if desired. Or serve unadorned with whipped cream on the side. Rarely is any of this intensely chocolate dessert left over.

EIGHT

BONEFISH FEVER IN QUINTANA ROO

March

CEVICHE

◆

PESCADA CON CREMA YUCATECA (RED SNAPPER WITH SOUR CREAM, OLIVES, AND RED BELL PEPPER SAUCE)

◆

JELLIED GUACAMOLE SALAD

◆

MAYACAMAS NAPA VALLEY CHARDONNAY

◆

MANGO SHERBET

In a sense, boarding the plane for this part of the Yucatán Peninsula is like stepping into a time machine. The twentieth-century bustle of the Cozumel airport fades away as the plane turns out over the Mexican Caribbean, and within twenty-five minutes one is circling over the ancient and intriguing world of the Mayan civilization. There are more ruins and dead cities in this part of the world than there are inhabited ones.

The little plane roars over Boca Paila Lodge on the shore and as it circles the landing strip, one can see the immense mangrove-dotted flats stretching for miles behind the sandy strip of beach front. There are myriad bonefish cruising around in there, just waiting for you! This is where the unconvinced become frenzied devotees of the maddening ritual of catching bonefish on a fly rod.

Most appropriately, all the buildings at Boca Paila are Mayan cottages, the perfect dwelling for the area. There are concessions to comfort, if not authenticity, in the form of concrete floors and tiled bathrooms, but the roofs are all coconut-palm thatched and supported by intricately placed poles and saplings. These buildings survive hurricanes, and archaeologists have discovered evidence of similar buildings that stood almost forty-five hundred years ago in what is now Belize. They are works of art in themselves, and they convey their message immediately: You are not in Detroit, or Sheboygan, or Nashville; you're in Quintana Roo.

Señora Gonzales presides over the kitchen from which issues Huevos Rancheros, Ceviche, and Pescada con Crema, among many other savory dishes. Mix up a Margarita before you serve the Ceviche as an appetizer, and try to imagine yourself overlooking a white sand beach stretching away to the horizon.

Ceviche

SERVES 8

Cut fish into cubes ½ inch square and put them into a large glass or ceramic bowl. Do not use metal. Pour the lemon and lime juice over the fish and stir to coat all cubes well. The juice should cover all the fish, because this "cooks" it. Let stand at room temperature for at least 1 hour or in the refrigerator for 3 hours.

In addition to the vegetables mentioned above, hot peppers can be added if you wish. I happen to dislike first courses that paralyze my taste buds, but if you are used to it, by all means add them.

The fish will be totally opaque when it is done. Chop all the vegetables and add to the fish with the seasonings. Mix well and chill 1 hour or overnight with a cover of plastic wrap.

Serve in individual seafood cocktail dishes or from a crystal bowl onto small rimmed plates. A few seafood crackers or some crusty bread and butter make nice accompaniments.

2 pounds barracuda, scallops, haddock, grey sole, or a mixture of these or any other white, firm-fleshed fish
1 cup lime juice (Key limes or Mexican limes, if possible)
1 cup fresh lemon juice .
½ cup chopped red onion, or chopped scallions (with green included)
¼ teaspoon minced garlic
1 teaspoon salt
Freshly ground pepper
1 red bell pepper, chopped
1 yellow bell pepper, chopped
1 green bell pepper, chopped
2 tablespoons minced cilantro leaves (or parsley)

Pescada con Crema Yucateca

3 pounds red snapper fillets,
  skinned

Flour to dredge fish

⅔ cup pimento-stuffed olives,
  halved lengthwise

4 fresh red bell peppers,
  chopped

1 garlic clove, minced

6 large fresh mushrooms, sliced

½ cup onions or scallions,
  chopped

2 cups sour cream

1 cup shredded sharp cheddar
  cheese

1 cup shredded Monterey Jack
  cheese

6 tablespoons butter

4 tablespoons oil

3 tablespoons fresh cilantro (or
  parsley) leaves, chopped

1 teaspoon salt

Freshly ground white pepper to
  taste

The catch in the Yucatán is mainly bonefish, an occasional tarpon, and the rare, exciting permit. All of these fish are released, however; none of them are considered table fish. In the event that one should run into a school of red snapper, a few are kept for eating. Any firm, white-fleshed fish is suitable for this recipe; just be sure the fillets are ½ inch thick.

Preheat oven to 350°.

Melt 5 tablespoons butter and 2 tablespoons oil in a large skillet. Dredge the snapper fillets in flour and sauté them in batches over medium-high heat for just 2 minutes on each side. Remove from pan and set aside on a large plate.

In the same skillet sauté the onions, garlic, and peppers for 3 or 4 minutes, adding the remaining oil and butter. Add the mushrooms and cook 2 or 3 minutes longer. Do not allow the vegetables to brown. Remove the vegetables from the pan with a slotted spoon, and discard the liquid. Transfer the vegetables to a large bowl and add the sour cream. Add salt and freshly ground white pepper to taste.

Butter a shallow 9 by 13-inch baking dish and arrange the fish fillets in the bottom. Place the vegetables evenly over them, using a slotted spoon to drain off any liquid that has accumulated in the bowl. Scatter the halved olives among the vegetables, and top with the shredded cheeses. This casserole may be made ahead to this point and heated later.

Bake in the preheated oven for 10 minutes, until the fish is just cooked through and the cheese is melted. Do not overcook. Serve immediately from the casserole with the chopped cilantro or parsley sprinkled on top.

Jellied Guacamole Salad

Soften gelatin in the cold water in a small bowl, then pour the warm chicken stock over it and stir until dissolved.

Peel, seed, and roughly cut up the avocados and place them in a food processor and purée with the onion juice, lemon juice, Tabasco, and salt. If doing this by hand, mash the avocadoes with a fork until they are smooth, add the seasonings, and mix well.

Add the gelatin and chicken stock mixture to the processor and run until it is well incorporated into the avocado mixture. If proceeding without a food processor, whisk the liquid into the mashed avocado and make sure there are no lumps of avocado left.

Rinse individual custard cups or one large mold in cold water and shake out the excess water before pouring the guacamole into them. Chill until firm, at least 2 or 3 hours. Unmold onto a serving dish and garnish with the lettuce leaves, tomato, and cucumber wedges. If you wish, drizzle mayonnaise thinned with a little lemon juice over the salads before serving them.

2 medium-to-large ripe avocados (You will need 2 cups mashed pulp.)
1 packet unflavored gelatin
½ cup cold water
1 cup warm chicken stock (Canned broth is all right.)
2 tablespoons lemon juice
1 teaspoon salt
Dash Tabasco sauce
1 teaspoon onion juice
Lettuce leaves, cucumber wedges, and tomato wedges for garnish
6 tablespoons mayonnaise thinned with 2 teaspoons lemon juice (optional)

Mango Sherbet

MAKES 1½ QUARTS

Mangoes are so delicious. It's well worth haunting your produce manager in the local supermarket to find out when they will be available. Buy a lot and make sherbet. It will keep for months in the freezer. Or, you can make mango purée and freeze it and then make fresh batches of sherbet throughout the year as you need it.

3 cups mango purée (5 or 6 medium mangoes—make sure they are ripe)

3 tablespoons fresh lemon juice

2 egg whites

¾ cup water

¾ cup sugar

Dissolve sugar in the water in a heavy-bottomed saucepan. Boil for 5 minutes. Remove from heat and cool.

Hold the stem end of the mango in your hand and rest the other end on a cutting board. With a sharp knife, cut through the skin from top to bottom in 4 or 5 places. Then peel the skin down as you would with a banana. The mango seed is large and flat, so it is best to slice flesh from the seed lengthwise. Purée the peeled, seeded mango in a food processor, blender, or food mill. Combine the mango purée, lemon juice, and sugar syrup and mix well.

Beat the egg whites until soft peaks form and carefully fold some of them into the purée to lighten it. Reverse the procedure and pour the purée into the remaining egg whites and fold it in thoroughly. Spoon the mixture into the chilled canister of your ice cream machine and freeze according to the manufacturer's instructions, or freeze in ice cube trays in the refrigerator.

When you can't find mangoes, or run out of frozen purée, use ripe peaches instead. It's not as heavenly in flavor, but it will do until the next shipment of mangoes arrives.

NINE

CAMPING OUT WITH ONLY NINETEEN SERVANTS IN UTTAR PRADESH

March

RED JUNGLE FOWL CARDAMOM

◆

GOLDEN RICE

◆

FRESH SPINACH WITH SAUTÉED RED PEPPERS

◆

STERLING NAPA VALLEY MERLOT

◆

SELF-COMPOSED CHEESECAKE

Our host, who can afford to be a perfectionist in matters small and large, had sent eighteen people, food supplies, two kerosene refrigerators, bedding, linen, dishes, cooking utensils (including a portable tandoori oven), cases of cartridges, fishing tackle, and other sundry items ahead to set up camp and get the wrinkles out one week before we departed from his home in New Delhi. He had leased two shooting blocks about two hundred miles east of the capital city, near the border of Tibet. Later, we would fish for the golden mahseer in Corbett National Park where the single largest population of Indian tigers reside.

On the appointed day we left New Delhi in the Mercedes followed by the senior family retainer in the Land Rover with the cases of wine and liquor and the family's black Lab. We stopped halfway and had a cool drink while the rugs were spread on the ground and the luncheon was set out.

At camp, our quarters were a large concrete house that was erected for the British superintendent engineer when the railway lines were built. It had four bedrooms, sitting room, dining room, and kitchen, all with fireplaces, and a bathroom with a flush toilet and shower. A verandah ran the length of the house and every evening a huge fire would be built in front and the chairs placed around it. The bar would be set up nearby, and a long table was placed as an outdoor buffet, complete with tablecloth and candles.

The Maharajah and Maharani of Patalia joined our hunt with three of their staff who, in short order, set up a tent with three peaked roofs from which fluttered the flags of the once royal and still rich and powerful house of Punjab.

A driven-bird shoot in northern India is not only a test of skill for the average North American hunter, but it also seems to be a test of his grasp on reality. First come the monkeys, chattering excitedly as they swing on vines through the trees, scampering with fantastic speed on all fours, screaming and gesticulating. Some clutch babies as they rush away from the beaters, through and around the unmoving line of guns. Next, the peacocks soar overhead with their immense tails flowing behind them. They are huge, majestic, powerful, and wild, which means they do not fly like the peacock one sees on a lawn in the southern United States. They are as different from ornamental peacocks as wild turkeys are different from their pitiful, overstuffed domestic brethren. It is not allowed to shoot the peacock—the national symbol of India.

Mixed with these, our quarry, the red jungle fowl, dart like so many berserk rockets. They are very sporty targets, and it's hard to remember that this bird is the forefather of *all* domestic chickens in the world. (It must be emphasized that we are not talking about shooting the rare grey jungle fowl, well known to and coveted by fly tiers. These birds are strictly protected, and woe to any simpleminded soul who tries to get through customs with even one grey junglecock feather in his possession, much less tries to shoot one.)

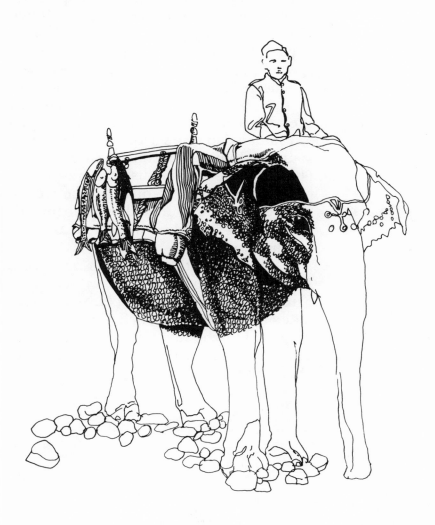

Camping Out with Only Nineteen Servants

At a huge shout from the beaters the line of guns prepares for a wild boar crashing through the underbrush toward them. An occasional coliche pheasant (fair game) adds a little more variety to the scene, and downriver the wild elephants are calmly spraying water over themselves during their midmorning bath.

It all looks like a scene arranged by Cecil B. DeMille, but then to Western eyes much of India does. You begin to realize that this place really exists with your first view of the supreme Taj Mahal, or of a train with three hundred people clinging to the outside or sitting on the roof as it rolls through the countryside (because it's too crowded to get inside). It's all dramatic, exotic, and vibrant.

Three or four days after the shoot, after the birds have been properly hung, they appear on the buffet in a delicious cardamom sauce. The following recipe can be used with domestic chicken or pheasant if you don't happen to have any red jungle fowl on hand. This is a special presentation of poultry because the two most expensive and precious spices in the world are used in it: saffron and cardamom. I have adapted the dish to Western palates by toning down the spiciness. Northern Indians do not eat their food as hotly seasoned as southern Indians, but they do use an enormous variety of spices in the same dish, all freshly ground and prepared in a *masala*, which can be wet or dry. In this case, the masala is mixed with yogurt (thus making it wet), and it is used both as the marinade and the base for the sauce.

Please note that the birds must be marinated for 1 hour before cooking. This will give you time to prepare your *ghee* (browned, clarified butter), which will take 45 minutes. Clarified butter can be used in place of ghee, but the nutty flavor it lends to the dish will be absent. More about this later. Now prepare the masala for the marinade.

Red Jungle Fowl (or Chicken) Cardamom

SERVES 6 TO 8

Two 3-pound frying chickens,
  cut up
Salt

MASALA

An Indian hostess would grind the seeds in a mortar thus releasing their full flavor. By all means, do so at this point if you want a stronger flavor. My method is less work and, admittedly, less authentic. I put all the masala ingredients into a food processor and let the machine run for 2 minutes. The cardamom seeds and fennel seeds will be bruised enough to release their flavor, but will still appear as little black lumps in the yogurt. At this point I put the mixture through a sieve and remove the lumps and discard them, reserving the yogurt mixture in a small bowl.

Rub salt into the skin of the chicken pieces and, using a brush or a rubber spatula, spread the masala over them and set aside at room temperature in a large roasting pan or on a cookie sheet for 1 hour.

16 cardamom seeds
2 tablespoons fresh, peeled,
  roughly chopped ginger root
1 teaspoon fennel seeds
Pinch cayenne pepper
1 tablespoon finely chopped
  garlic
1 cup unflavored yogurt

GHEE

Place the butter in a heavy-bottomed pan and melt it over medium heat. Stir it a bit, but do not let it brown at this point. When melted, turn the heat to high for just a moment and let the surface foam. Stir once, and immediately turn the heat to the lowest possible setting. (If you are using an electric stove, remove the butter from the heat until the burner cools.) Leave the butter on the burner, uncovered, and do not stir for 45 minutes. The milk solids will sink to the bottom and brown, and the butter on top should be transparent.

½ pound unsalted butter

Camping Out with Only Nineteen Servants

Pour the resulting clear liquid butter through a fine sieve lined with a linen towel or large paper coffee filter. The ghee is now ready to use. Store any left over in a jar or crock with a lid. It can be kept at room temperature safely for 3 months without turning rancid. (This is a useful thing to know in a warm country where kitchens do not have refrigerators.)

½ teaspoon saffron threads
3 tablespoons boiling water
½ cup of the ghee you prepared
One 3-inch cinnamon stick
2 whole cloves
2 cups finely chopped onions
½ cup cold water

Put the saffron threads into a small bowl and cover them with the boiling water.

In a large heavy-bottomed frying or roasting pan with a lid, heat the ghee and drop in the cinnamon stick and cloves, and stir until they are coated. Add the chopped onions and cook them for 7 or 8 minutes, until they are golden in color. Do not brown them.

Place the pieces of meat on top of the onions, pour in any remaining masala, and add the saffron and its liquid. Cook over medium heat, turning the chicken pieces over so that they become colored on both sides but not brown. Stir in the ½ cup cold water, turn the heat up, and bring all to a boil.

Lower the heat, cover the pan with foil, and place the lid on top. This dish can be made ahead up to this point and refrigerated until you want to serve it.

Cook over moderate to low heat for 20 to 25 minutes. Remove the chicken pieces from the pan and transfer them to a heated serving dish. Discard the cinnamon stick and cloves and pour the remaining sauce over the chicken before serving.

Golden Rice

SERVES 8

1½ cups long grain rice (Basmati rice is most authentic.)
12 cups water
1 teaspoon ground turmeric
3 tablespoons butter (or to taste)
6 chicken bouillon cubes

Rinse the rice in a sieve with cold running water. Place it in a large pot with the 12 cups water and the chicken bouillon cubes. Bring to a boil, then lower heat and simmer for 45 minutes. Add chicken broth or water if it gets dry and starts sticking, ½ cup at a time. All the water should be absorbed when it is done.

If there is any excess liquid, drain the rice after it is cooked. Mix the ground turmeric into the softened butter and stir it into the hot rice. Serve immediately.

Fresh Spinach with Sautéed Red Peppers

SERVES 8

Sauté the julienned peppers in the butter in a heavy-bottomed frying pan for 10 minutes. Boil the spinach for 3 or 4 minutes, drain, and place in a deep heated dish. Pour the pepper strips on top and add salt and pepper to taste.

This vegetable adds the necessary color and texture contrast to the chicken and rice. If you hate spinach, use any green vegetable and garnish it with sautéed red pepper strips. The plates will look incomparably dull without this dash of enlivening color.

2 pounds fresh spinach (or 4 packages frozen)
3 tablespoons butter
3 red bell peppers, seeded and cut into julienne strips
Salt and pepper

Self-Composed Cheesecake

SERVES 6 TO 8

This dessert is not an authentic Indian recipe, but who cares? It's the name that counts—there never was a more self-composed people. The real reason I named this dessert so is because this clever cake bakes its own crust as it cooks. It's simple to make, looks like you've slaved away, and tastes great after spicy food.

Preheat oven to 350°.

Put the cream cheese, eggs, almond extract, and sugar into a food processor, or use an electric mixer. Run the machine for a minute or two until all the ingredients are blended well and there are no lumps of cheese left.

Pour the mixture into an 8-inch pie plate (ungreased), put it into the preheated oven, and bake it for 30 minutes. It will be golden brown and beautifully puffed up. Remove it from the oven and let it cool for 15 minutes. Reduce the oven heat to 325°.

As the cake cools, the center will fall and create a depression. The browned outside edge will then be-

Two 8-ounce packages cream cheese, softened
3 large eggs
1 teaspoon almond extract
⅓ cup sugar

TOPPING

1 cup sour cream
3 tablespoons sugar
1 teaspoon vanilla

come a raised crust around the rim of the cake. Fill the depression inside the rim of the crust with the topping mixture. Return the cake to the 325° oven for 10 minutes. Remove when done and cool for at least 1 hour. Chill in the refrigerator before serving. It's the most elegant dessert you'll ever make with so little effort.

TEN

A PICNIC IN PATAGONIA

March

TROUT CHIMEHUIN ROASTED IN THE COALS OR FILET MIGNON
ON THE ROCKS

◆

TOMATO-CHEESE PIE

◆

ASSORTED OLIVES, PICKLES, AND CRUDITÉS

◆

ARGENTINIAN WHITE WINE

◆

PATAGONIAN PASTELES

The southern part of Argentina is my favorite place to fish. Perhaps it's because I have big feet that I feel so much at home there. This makes sense because Patagonia means "Land of the Big Feet."

There are other reasons as well, such as the variety of streams to fish: the Colloncura, the Chimehuin, the Majello, and the Caleufu to name just a few. In addition, there is the awesome beauty of the Andes Mountains and their lakes, the desert-floor wildlife (not least, the rhea), the sight of gauchos riding gravely by, tipping their hats, and a wonderful little pension where we stay in St. Martin de los Andes.

It's called "La Raclette." This is ski country, after all, and raclette is served every night during the cocktail hour. Even though this dish is of Swiss origin, it fits perfectly in the mountains of South America. It consists of tiny boiled potatoes, melted Gruyère scraped off a huge wheel of cheese that is placed in front of the fire, tiny pickled onions, and cornichons. It's a toothsome hors d'oeuvre in the cool mountain evenings, just as it would be for a winter dinner in front of the fire at home. In larger portions it could be expanded into the whole dinner itself, or it could be used at a relaxed Sunday luncheon.

Speaking of luncheon, here is a great way to cook fish at streamside, which was introduced to us at a midday picnic in Patagonia.

Trout Chimehuin

1 large sheet of heavy-duty aluminum foil for each serving

Salt and pepper

1 tablespoon butter for each serving (If it's very warm weather, take a small plastic bottle of olive oil instead.)

1 lemon wedge per serving

1 small tomato, cut into wedges, per serving

½ green bell pepper, cut into ½-inch strips, per serving

½ small onion, cut into wedges or sliced, per serving

1½-pound trout or equal portion of fillet from a larger fish (which you will catch on the stream before luncheon) per serving

Paper towels to dry fish after cleaning it in the stream

Pocket knife or paring knife to clean the fish

Start a fire and let it burn down to a bed of hot ashes and small coals.

Clean the fish, or fillet it if it is over 1½ pounds. Dry it as much as possible with the paper towels. Place the fish in the center of the foil, add the vegetables and salt and pepper, and put the butter or oil on top of them. Try to keep the packet as flat as possible and fold the ends of the foil up and over the seam, keeping the seam up, so as not to lose the oil or butter.

Place the package of foil and fish in the middle of the coals and roast approximately 4 minutes on each side or 5 minutes on each side if the fish is particularly thick.

Remove from the fire with tongs or a forked stick and open the foil. Eat it right from the foil or remove to a plate.

Filet Mignon on the Rocks (an alternate)

If you are not absolutely sure you will catch trout, or if you're fishing a river where they should be released, take along a thick slice of fillet of beef for each serving.

When you build your fire, ring it closely with some clean flat stones from the river. In 20 to 25 minutes, when the fire has burned down, haul the stones out of the fire with a stick and place a slice of filet on each one. The meat will cook beautifully right on the heated rock. Leave it about 5 minutes and turn it to cook for another 5 minutes. There are no grills or pans to tote and no messy black utensils to clean up. It's a dramatic and very useful method of cooking we learned in Patagonia from our good friend and lifelong resident of the area, Douglas Reid.

Tomato-Cheese Pie

SERVES 6 TO 8

Preheat oven to 350°.

Dredge the tomato slices in 2 tablespoons flour and brown lightly in butter, turning once. Drain on paper towels and set aside.

Combine the remaining 1 tablespoon flour, the cottage cheese, sour cream, eggs, green onion, parsley, salt, Worcestershire sauce, and basil.

Arrange half the cheese slices over bottom of crust. Spoon in half the cottage cheese mixture and cover with the tomato slices. Repeat with the remaining cheese slices and cottage cheese mixture and sprinkle with Parmesan cheese.

Bake for 30 to 35 minutes, or until set. (Test with a knife inserted in the center. If it comes out clean, the pie is done.) Cool 15 minutes before serving.

This pie can be made in small individual pie pans or tart shells. It travels much better, in fact, if it is made into tarts. Leave them right in the pans to pack for the picnic. They taste better cold or at room temperature than they do warm, thus making them ideal for picnic purposes.

Instead of a salad, take along an assortment of olives, pickles, and fresh vegetables cut into bite-sized pieces.

2 or 3 tomatoes, 10 slices total
3 tablespoons flour
2 tablespoons butter
1 cup large-curd cottage cheese
1 cup sour cream
3 eggs, slightly beaten
¼ cup thinly sliced green onions
2 tablespoons chopped parsley
1 teaspoon salt
1 teaspoon Worcestershire sauce
½ teaspoon basil
4 to 6 slices good cheddar cheese
1 unbaked pie shell (see recipe for Onion Tart)
⅓ cup grated Parmesan cheese

Patagonian Pasteles, or Quince-filled Crescents

1½ cups all-purpose flour
½ teaspoon double-acting
    baking powder
½ teaspoon salt
½ cup butter (1 stick)
3 tablespoons cold water
1 cup plus 2 tablespoons
    prepared quince paste or
    quince jam
Lemon wedges
Confectioner's sugar

These are an Argentinian favorite. If you can't find prepared quince paste, use a good quince jam or marmalade and squeeze a wedge of lemon over it before filling the pasteles.

Preheat oven to 350°. Put the flour, baking powder, and salt in a food processor bowl. Run a second or so to mix and then add the butter, 1 tablespoon or pat at a time. Add the water and run the machine for 5 or 6 seconds, until a ball forms.

If doing this by hand, cut the butter into the dry ingredients and add water, a few teaspoonfuls at a time. Knead the dough gently until it can be gathered into a ball.

On a floured board, roll out the dough into a large circle about ⅛ inch thick. With a 4-inch, round, cookie cutter, cut the dough into as many rounds as you can. Then gather the scraps together, reform into a ball, roll out again, and cut the rounds. Repeat until you have used all the dough.

Put 1 tablespoon of the quince paste or jam into the center of each round. Squeeze a few drops of lemon juice on at this time. Brush a little cold water around the edge of the round, fold in half over the filling, and seal shut by crimping with your fingers or by pressing with the tines of a fork.

Place the cookies on a lightly greased cookie sheet and bake in the center of the preheated oven for 15 to 20 minutes. They should be golden brown. Remove with a spatula to cool on a wire rack and dust lightly with confectioner's sugar before serving. This is one of a few desserts that taste good with a dry white wine. To complete your meal, be sure to try an Argentinian white wine; they are excellent.

ELEVEN

DINNER FOR JUDGES AND OFFICIALS THE EVENING BEFORE THE FIELD TRIAL

March

Hot Cream of Mustard Soup

◆

Sautéed Quail on Toast

◆

Quail Liver Mousse garnished with French Fried Parsley

◆

Hashed-in-Cream Potatoes Extraordinaire

◆

Baby Bibb Lettuce with Fresh Peas

◆

Chateau Montelena Napa and Alexander Valley Chardonnay

◆

Oranges in White Wine with Ginger

At one such dinner quite a few years ago, the owner of the plantation where the field trial was to be held the next day stood up to say a few words. He apologized in advance for not having many quail on his plantation that year. The following day the sixteen best pointers in the area found one hundred coveys on his place. The day after that he fired his dog handler.

The Georgia-Florida field trial is an important event for dog owners, handlers, and, of course, the dogs. They are usually English Pointers with an occasional English Setter who has the nose and the stamina to compete with the big-going pointers. The dogs need about eight thousand acres for one day's competition.

A brace of entrants is put down every half hour. Each dog has exactly thirty minutes to find as many coveys as he can. A course has been determined in advance and the handler must keep his dog on it or suffer sure elimination from the prize-winner's circle. There is a local judge and an out-of-town judge, plus timekeepers, field marshals, and a gallery of several hundred people. They are all on horseback or in shooting wagons drawn by mules. Some use jeeps.

It is quite a spectacle as this large entourage moves out across the fields with horses snorting and mules braying. It looks like a turn of the century Russian army moving into the spring campaign. It's also a very sociable affair because all these people get together in one place only once a year.

GAME IN SEASON

If you are feeling sorry for the quail, don't. No one is shooting at them that day; a shot is fired into the air at each point merely for the dog's satisfaction and to demonstrate that the point was productive.

Cream of Mustard Soup

SERVES 8

Melt the butter in a heavy-bottomed pan, add the flour, and allow to bubble for 3 minutes. Gradually add stock and milk; cook and whisk until smooth and slightly thickened. Remove from the heat and season with the salt, pepper, and onion juice.

Combine egg yolks, mustard, and cream. Whisk in ½ cup of the hot soup, then return to the rest of the soup. Reheat but do not boil. Adjust the seasonings to taste.

Garnish with a sprinkle of chopped parsley on top.

This is a subtly flavored, elegant soup. It may be served hot or chilled.

4 tablespoons each butter and flour (potato or rice flour, if possible)
5 cups chicken stock (Homemade is best, canned chicken consommé will do.)
2½ cups homogenized milk, scalded
1 teaspoon salt
½ teaspoon white pepper, freshly ground
3 teaspoons onion juice
4 egg yolks, beaten
8 tablespoons prepared Dijon mustard
6 tablespoons heavy cream
Minced parsley for garnish

Sautéed Quail

ALLOW 2 QUAIL OR 1 CORNISH GAME HEN PER PERSON

Split the kitchen-ready birds up the breast with game shears. Spread out and crack the back just the way you should *not* do with a new book. The meat will lie flatter, and it will take less time to cook with the breast split.

Melt 4 tablespoons of butter and 1 of oil in a sauté pan, and place the birds in the pan, skin side down. Keep on low heat and cook for approximately 4 minutes on each side. (Cook twice as long for the game hens.) The internal temperature when done should be 140° to 150° in the thickest part of the breast.

Remove the crusts from thin-sliced Howley White Bread (*which see*). Cut the slices in half to make triangles. Toast the bread and spread with Quail Liver Mousse. Place the cooked birds skin side up over the toast slices. Garnish with French Fried Parsley.

Quail Liver Mousse

MAKES SIX 4-OUNCE RAMEKINS

½ pound quail livers and hearts (Have whoever cleans the quail save these and freeze them until you have enough. Chicken liver may be substituted in this recipe, but the flavor is not as subtle as quail liver.)
1 tablespoon butter
1 tablespoon oil
¾ cup heavy cream
2 large eggs
Scant ½ teaspoon freshly ground nutmeg
½ teaspoon salt
½ teaspoon freshly ground black pepper

Preheat oven to 350°.

Clean and trim the quail or chicken livers, removing any dark spots. Sauté the livers in the butter and oil over medium-low heat for about 3 minutes. Watch them and stir occasionally because they are so small that they burn easily. Purée them in a food processor or food mill, or mash them thoroughly with a fork. Place the purée into a large bowl and add the heavy cream and eggs. Add the nutmeg, salt, and pepper. The mixture should have the consistency of thick cream.

Pour into small, buttered, ovenproof ramekins or custard cups and place these in a bain-marie. Cook gently for about 25 minutes on top of the stove over low heat. Then place the bain-marie into the preheated oven for 15 minutes. A silver knife should come out clean when inserted into the cooked mousse if it is done.

Cool and refrigerate with a cover of foil or cling wrap. Remove from refrigerator 1 hour before serving and bring to room temperature before spreading on the toast. If you are using this as an hors d'oeuvre, unmold and garnish.

This is a delicately flavored mousse. It can be used as described in this recipe, or it can be served as the ultimate first course with one whole truffle on top (as they serve pâté at Roger Lamazere in Paris). Or it can be presented as a luncheon with Sour French Cornichons (*which see*), a green salad, and French bread.

It can be wrapped in plastic wrap and then foil (in the ramekin), and frozen. It will keep at least 3 months frozen. Defrost completely before serving.

French Fried Parsley

This decoration is definitely meant to be eaten.

Wash and dry the parsley. Sprinkle it with milk, then dust with flour. Fry in any good vegetable oil at 425° for 1 minute. Do not overcook; the parsley should stay green. Drain on paper towels and lightly sprinkle with salt. This is also excellent with fish.

2 bunches curly parsley
½ cup skim milk
½ cup flour
Salt

Hashed-in-Cream Potatoes Extraordinaire

SERVES 8

These potatoes are vastly different from the gooey mass that usually appears under this name. This dish is truly delicious; the potatoes are still crunchy and the cream is very delicately flavored with the sautéed onion.

Chop the potatoes finely in a food processor or by hand. If using a food processor, use the on-off technique and watch carefully. Stop the minute most of the potatoes are the size of a pumpkin seed. You do *not* want puréed potatoes. Finish any large chunks of potato by hand chopping.

Place the potatoes in a sieve and wash off all the starch in cold running water. Let the water run through them for 3 or 4 minutes, stirring them occasionally to make sure all the starch is out. This is a very important step; it is why the potatoes do not get gooey.

Drain well and place the potatoes in a towel and squeeze out all the water. Put them in the top of a double boiler and add the cream, salt and pepper, and sautéed onion. Stir well and cover. Simmer for 3 hours, stirring occasionally. Check the water in the bottom half of the double boiler periodically to make sure it doesn't go dry.

This can be made a day ahead of time and stored in the refrigerator. Reheat in a double boiler for about 20 minutes before serving, stirring occasionally.

2½ pounds white potatoes, peeled
1 pint whipping cream
½ teaspoon salt
½ teaspoon white pepper
1 tablespoon finely minced onion sautéed in butter

Baby Bibb Lettuce with Fresh Peas

SERVES 8

6 tablespoons butter
½ cup chopped scallions
10 small heads Bibb lettuce, with large outer leaves removed
4 pounds green peas, shelled, or 4 packages frozen tiny peas
Salt to taste
½ cup chicken stock (Canned broth is all right.)
1 tablespoon chopped parsley
Freshly ground pepper to taste

Melt the butter in a large heavy saucepan. Add the scallions and sauté briefly. Add the lettuce and peas and sprinkle with salt. Add the stock, cover, and cook over low heat for 20 minutes or until the peas are tender. Remove from the heat, add the parsley and pepper, and serve in a deep bowl.

Oranges in White Wine with Ginger

SERVES 8

10 navel oranges
1⅓ cups dry white wine (This dish will be as good as the wine you use.)
One 10-ounce jar preserved ginger in syrup, undrained
1 cup fresh orange juice
2 tablespoons fresh lemon juice
1½ tablespoons superfine sugar
¼ cup diced candied ginger

Remove the peel (without the membrane) from 2 oranges using a vegetable peeler. Cut into the thinnest possible julienne. Wrap the peel tightly in foil or plastic and refrigerate. Peel the rest of the oranges, removing the white membrane. Slice thinly and place them in a serving bowl.

Combine the wine, preserved ginger (with syrup), orange and lemon juices, and sugar in a food processor and process using on-off technique until the ginger is finely chopped. Pour over the orange slices and toss gently. Cover and refrigerate for at least 4 hours. This may be made a day ahead of time.

Before serving, sprinkle with the reserved orange peel julienne and ¼ cup finely diced candied ginger. This is a very refreshing, light dessert and sure to be a hit with ginger lovers.

TWELVE

AN EASTER TREAT

April

Salmon Koulebiaka

Fresh Steamed Asparagus with Quick Hollandaise Sauce

Wilted Niçoise Salad

◆

Pouilly-Fuissé

◆

Madame Begue's Creamed Soda Crackers

Salmon Koulebiaka

SERVES 6

This is the White Russian counterpart of the Moroccan *Pastilla*, the French *Pâté en Croute*, or the English Porkpie or Pasty. The Russian emigrés who in 1917 fled the Revolution to Nice, France, have made that city famous for its Koulebiaka during the spring festival season. It can be made with any firm-fleshed fish, but it is especially good when made with fresh salmon. Try it for a change from the traditional Easter ham or leg of lamb. The recipe can also be used for a luncheon with just a tossed green salad.

Preheat oven to 400°.

Put the first 4 ingredients into a food processor and run the machine for 30 seconds, or until the dough forms into a ball. Remove, roll into a ball, wrap in plastic or foil, and allow to rest in the refrigerator for 10 minutes. Or mix by hand and refrigerate.

Make sure the cooked rice is dry. Heat it in a skillet on low heat and stir to dry, if necessary. Skin and bone the fish slices. Coarsely chop the hard-boiled eggs. Chop the parsley and dill.

Roll out the dough on a floured piece of waxed paper (moisten the counter with a wet sponge and the paper will stick in place). Roll into a rough rectangle at least 12 inches wide and about 14 inches long. In the center place ½ of the cooked rice pressed flat but kept in the middle third of the dough.

With a rubber spatula spread half the sour cream over the rice and put the sliced salmon on top. Cover the salmon with the remaining half of the rice and sour cream, and sprinkle the chopped egg on top. Season with salt and pepper, and half of the dill and parsley.

Fold the dough sides over each other on top of the filling and moisten the edges with water to seal. Roll or fold up the ends and seal them with a little water brushed onto the dough edges. You should have a neat, rectangular package with a double dough layer on the top.

2 sticks (½ pound) butter, cut into pats
1 teaspoon salt
2 cups flour
½ cup ice water
1½ pounds fresh salmon (or any firm-fleshed fish), cut into 4 thick slices
1½ cups sour cream
⅔ cup long grain rice, cooked
2 large eggs, hard-boiled and chopped
½ teaspoon salt
¼ teaspoon freshly ground black pepper
Dorure (1 egg yolk beaten together with 1 teaspoon water and a pinch of salt)
½ cup fresh parsley, minced
½ cup fresh dill, minced
1 bunch watercress for garnish
4 tablespoons butter, melted

Grease a cookie sheet, spread it with foil, and grease the foil. Slide the package of dough on its piece of waxed paper onto the cookie sheet, turning it over so the double layer of dough is on the bottom. Brush the top with the egg and water mixture.

Cut a 1-inch diameter hole in the center of the top with a sharp knife and prick the surface with a fork in several places.

Bake in the preheated oven for 15 minutes, then lower the heat to 350° and bake about 10 minutes longer. When the dough is golden brown, it is done.

Melt the 4 tablespoons of butter and combine with the remaining chopped dill and parsley. Just before serving, pour this into the round hole you made on top of the Koulebiaka.

Place on a warm serving platter and surround with watercress and perhaps a few of your most beautifully decorated Easter eggs. To serve, slice with a sharp knife dipped in hot water.

An Easter Treat

Fresh Steamed Asparagus

2 pounds fresh asparagus,
washed, drained, with reedy
ends cut off

It's best to cook asparagus upright on a rack over boiling water in a covered steamer especially designed for it, or you could use a French potato steamer that allows the asparagus to stand vertically. Thicker stalks are usually more tender than thin, stringy ones. Check the bottom of the stalks with a paring knife after 6 minutes of steaming—if it pierces them easily, they're done. Asparagus shouldn't be limp.

Because the salmon tends to be rich, you may want to simply dress the asparagus with butter and salt and pepper. If you want to make a quick Hollandaise however, here's a fast recipe. It can be made ahead of time and stored in a thermos that has been rinsed in very hot water to heat the inside. This way you won't have to worry about curdling problems while it's waiting.

Quick Hollandaise Sauce

TO ACCOMPANY 2 POUNDS OF ASPARAGUS

1 cup (2 sticks) butter, melted
6 egg yolks at room
temperature (Immerse the
eggs in warm water for 10
minutes if you just took them
out of the refrigerator.)
4 tablespoons lemon juice
¼ teaspoon salt
Pinch white pepper

Put the egg yolks into a blender or whisk by hand. Add the lemon juice, salt, and pepper. With the machine running, or while whisking constantly, slowly pour the melted butter into the egg yolk mixture until it becomes thick and smooth. Pour into a heated thermos immediately and keep warm until serving time.

Wilted Niçoise Salad

SERVES 6

Wash the lettuce heads, keeping them whole. Place them upside down on paper towels to drain. Mix together the capers, olives, tomatoes, anchovies, and parsley, and drop it by spoonfuls among the lettuce leaves. If the heads of lettuce don't stand upright cut a little off the heart on the bottom to make them level.

Melt the butter in a stock pot or soup pot large enough to hold all of the lettuce heads in 1 layer. Add the olive oil, garlic, and thyme. Place over low heat and simmer for about 3 minutes to slightly wilt the lettuce and warm it through. Put on heated plates or a serving dish and ladle the braising liquid sparingly over the top. Sprinkle on a little salt and freshly ground pepper to taste.

6 small heads Bibb lettuce
30 niçoise olives
3 tomatoes, finely diced
2 tablespoons capers, drained
12 anchovy fillets, chopped finely
2 tablespoons fresh parsley, chopped
3 tablespoons butter
1½ tablespoons garlic, put through a garlic press
⅔ cup olive oil
2½ teaspoons fresh thyme, minced, or 1 teaspoon dried thyme
Salt and freshly ground pepper to taste

Madame Begue's Creamed Soda Crackers

SERVES 6 TO 8

Break the soda crackers into a large glass bowl. Warm the 2 cups of half-and-half over low heat for a few minutes. (To avoid scorching milk on the bottom of a pan, rinse the pan with *cold* water and shake out the excess before putting the milk into it.) Pour over the crackers and set aside.

Rinse the pan in cold water (again), shake out the excess water, and put in the 2 cups homogenized milk. Heat just to the scalding point, but do not boil. Beat the 3 egg whites until stiff and form egg-shaped blobs with an oval soup spoon. Drop these into the hot milk. (Dip the spoon into the hot milk first and then turn it through the egg whites, trying to make them goose-

Twenty four-inch square soda crackers
2 cups half-and-half
2 cups homogenized milk
3 eggs, separated
¼ cup sugar
1 teaspoon vanilla extract

egg shaped. The finished product will look more Easterish if you can do it.)

Turn the meringues over once with the spoon and cook about 20 seconds each. Take them out with the spoon and lay them over the crackers as they are cooked.

When all the meringues are finished, beat the egg yolks and pour ¼ cup of the hot milk over them while whisking constantly. Then pour the yolks into the remaining milk in the pan while whisking. Stir without stopping until the custard thickens. Be careful that it does not boil. Remove from the heat and add the ¼ cup sugar and the vanilla. Whisk well, let cool slightly (2 minutes), and pour around the meringues and over the crackers. Allow some of the white meringues to show off their beautiful egg shapes. Chill at least 1 hour before serving.

One more Easter note: If you have hard-boiled eggs galore, use them in Oeufs à la Tripe (*which see*).

THIRTEEN

DOVE SHOOTING IN THE MIDDLE ATLAS REGION

April

Dove Pastilla

◆

Rice Marrakchia

◆

White Acre Peas or Fresh Baby Lima Beans

◆

French Chablis

◆

Poached Pears in Red Wine with Vanilla Custard Sauce

Dove shooting in exotic Morocco. Images of Casablanca flit across the mind's eye. Ingrid Bergman, Humphrey Bogart, oppressive heat, smells, primitive, perhaps unsanitary lodgings, camels spitting, dust, squalor, right? Wrong!

The Gazelle D'or Hotel, near Taroudant, is so beautiful you'll wonder why you didn't honeymoon there. It was built as a private residence and is set in the midst of vast citrus groves. The eighty acres of flower gardens surrounding the bungalows and hotel spread like a vibrant Moroccan carpet in all directions. There are vistas of water splashing down stepped falls between tall cedar trees. The buildings are all stone, and if they had been less heroically built would probably have collapsed under the weight of the blossoming bougainvillea and espaliered lemon trees that cover them now.

The dove shooting is superb in this Middle Atlas Valley, and a popular local method of preparing them is in a *pastilla*. The turbaned and kaftan-clad waiters serve it between the soup course and the *couscous*. In the authentic Moroccan version the dove is moistened with a sweet custard, wrapped in strudel dough, and served with powdered sugar and cinnamon sprinkled on top. Our recipe has been adapted to suit the American taste for a less-sweet entrée.

This recipe can also be used as an hors d'oeuvre by cutting the dove breasts into fourths and making very small pastillas.

Dove Pastilla

SERVES 8 TO 10

Preheat oven to 375°.

Sauté the shallots and thyme in 1 tablespoon of the butter for 4 minutes. Do not allow them to brown. Set aside. Mince the almonds in a food processor or blender, then pour them into a small bowl and set it aside.

Wash and dry the mushrooms and mince them in a food processor (don't bother to wash and dry the processor bowl, the almond dust won't matter). Add the shallots and thyme to the mushrooms and process for 10 seconds.

Put this mixture into a heavy frying pan and stir for about 3 minutes over low heat to completely dry it out. Remove from the heat, add the minced almonds, allspice, salt and pepper, and mix well. Set aside. Sprinkle ½ cup flour over the halved dove breasts and rub it into the meat.

Melt ¼ pound butter and brush a cookie sheet with some of it. Place one sheet of the filo dough on the cookie sheet and brush it with melted butter. Repeat until you have six layers. (Be sure to cover remaining sheets of filo with a damp towel after you remove each one so the batch does not dry out.) Mound a large tablespoon of the mushroom mixture in the top corner of a filo sheet. Place a half dove breast on top. Cut off the dough to make a 6-inch square, and bring up the corners to wrap the dove in the dough. Invert on the cookie sheet so that the seams are down and repeat for each pastilla. Brush the tops with melted butter and bake in the preheated oven for 12 to 15 minutes.

The pastillas will be golden brown and crispy on the outside, and the dove light pink inside. The internal temperature should be 140° when done. Place on a heated platter, garnish with parsley or watercress, and serve immediately.

8 ounces filo pastry leaves (If you buy these frozen, defrost for at least 3 hours before using.)

10 mourning dove breasts, skinned (Make soup with the rest of the birds.)

¼ pound plus 1 tablespoon butter

3 shallots, minced

Leaves from two stalks of fresh thyme, or ½ teaspoon dried thyme

1 pound fresh mushrooms

½ cup blanched almonds, chopped fine

½ cup flour

¼ teaspoon allspice

1 teaspoon salt

Freshly ground pepper from green peppercorns

Rice Marrakchia

SERVES 8 TO 10

4 cups cooked long grain rice (2 cups uncooked)
1 onion, finely chopped
1 cup chopped pecans
½ cup pitted dried prunes, chopped
½ cup chopped dried apricots
1 tablespoon oil
4 tablespoons (½ stick) butter
1 teaspoon seasoned salt
2 to 3 tablespoons fresh chopped parsley

Boil the rice for 25 to 35 minutes, until it is tender but not mushy. Sauté the onion in the butter and oil in a heavy skillet for 5 to 7 minutes, until it is soft and transparent but not browned. Sprinkle the seasoned salt over the onions and add the pecans. Stir in the cooked rice and chopped fruits and parsley. Cover and let steam over very low heat for about 5 minutes until heated through before serving.

White Acre Peas

White acre peas, sometimes called field peas, are common in the southeastern United States. If you can't find them in your market, the closest substitute is fresh baby lima beans. Simply boil them until they are tender, and serve with plenty of butter and salt and pepper to taste. If you desire, you can place them in the center of a large, shallow bowl with the rice in a mounded ring around them, instead of presenting in separate serving dishes.

Poached Pears in Red Wine with Vanilla Custard Sauce

SERVES 8

This is an attractive dessert, especially if it is served in stemmed crystal or glass dessert dishes. The pears take on a beautiful color from the red wine.

Peel the pears with a potato peeler, being careful to leave the stems on. At the base of the pear, insert the potato peeler vertically and remove the core. It will come out easily as you rotate the peeler. Trim the base off flat with a knife so the pear will stand upright.

Put the remaining ingredients into a 1½-quart saucepan and bring to a boil. Lower the heat and slip the pears into the liquid with a spoon. Simmer gently for 45 minutes. Turn the pears with a spoon occasionally if the liquid doesn't completely cover them. Remove the pears from the liquid with a slotted spoon and let them drain on paper towels. Place the pears in individual serving dishes and spoon warm Vanilla Custard Sauce around them.

Both the pears and the sauce may be made several days ahead of time. Store the fruit in its poaching liquid in the refrigerator, with the sauce in a jar. The day you want to serve, remove the pears several hours ahead of time and bring them to room temperature. Reheat the sauce in a double boiler over *very low* heat, so the water is just hot—not boiling, or it will curdle. If it does start curdling, remove from the heat, drop an ice cube into it, and stir rapidly. If it still looks curdled quickly pour it into a blender or food processor and let machine run for 10 to 15 seconds, until the lumps are gone.

8 underripe Bartlett pears with stems attached
2 cups red table wine
1 cup water
½ cup sugar
1 tablespoon ground cinnamon, or 2 cinnamon sticks
½ teaspoon freshly ground nutmeg
6 whole cloves
Juice of 1 lemon
Peel of 1 lemon (Remove in strips with a potato peeler.)

VANILLA CUSTARD SAUCE

Combine the eggs, salt, and sugar. Add the scalded milk slowly, while whisking, and cook in the top of a double boiler until the mixture coats a spoon. Add vanilla and stir in thoroughly. Serve around poached pears immediately, or keep warm in a thermos until serving time if you are not cooking a day in advance.

2 eggs, slightly beaten
⅛ teaspoon salt
¼ cup sugar
2 cups milk, scalded
1 teaspoon vanilla extract

FOURTEEN

A BATTENKILL BANQUET

May

Steamed Fiddlehead Ferns or Fresh Asparagus

◆

Trout Soufflé with Sauce Sabayon

◆

Freemark Abbey Napa Valley Pinot Chardonnay

◆

Watercress Salad With Mustard Vinaigrette Dressing

◆

Tart Lemon Roulade

Steamed Fiddlehead Ferns

The first days of May in Vermont bring the Hendrickson hatch on the Battenkill—the fly fisher's delight. Along the riverbanks the fiddlehead ferns are just pushing their way through the sand. They are picked while still coiled in a tight circle. Steam or gently simmer them in water for 5 to 8 minutes and serve simply with butter and salt and pepper to taste. They should be crunchy and still bright green. Some markets have fresh fiddleheads in season, but if you can't find them in your area fresh asparagus is a good substitute.

The papery brown skins on the ferns must be removed. The best way to get most of them off is to put the just-picked fiddleheads directly into your landing net and hold it in a fast-moving riffle of the stream. The skins will float away downriver and there will be much less work in the kitchen. In any case, wash the skins off as soon as possible after picking, while they are dry and slip off easily. They tend to stick more tightly after being refrigerated.

Trout Soufflé with Sauce Sabayon

SERVES 6

This is without question my favorite fish recipe. I have only one suggestion to improve it: Release your trout and make this dish with sole, as is called for in the original French recipe.

I once had this dish on the menu for a dinner party when the power went out just a half hour before the guests were to arrive. The fish was ready to go into the oven so we had cold soup first, waiting for the lights to come on again. Then the salad was eaten—no power. I finally cooked it on trivets on top of the wood stove. It was delicious. The power came back on thirty minutes after the guests had left.

That's the week I threw out the electric stove and got one that worked with bottled gas. While I don't recommend cooking by the woodstove method, the incident does show how adaptable this recipe is.

TO POACH THE FISH

Preheat oven to 350°.

Place the fish in a buttered shallow baking dish, add wine and water, carrot, onion, and herbs. Cover with aluminum foil and poach in the preheated oven for 10 minutes.

Remove the fish from the liquid to a plate. Strain the liquid into a heavy-bottomed saucepan and reduce by boiling to ¼ cup. Set aside. This reduced liquid will be the base of your sauce.

1½ pounds skinned filets of sole
½ cup white wine
½ cup water
1 carrot, sliced
1 onion, sliced
Bouquet garni of 4 sprigs fresh thyme (or 1 teaspoon dried thyme), 1 bayleaf, and 4 sprigs of fresh parsley

SOUFFLÉ

Reset the oven to 425°.

Scald the milk in a heavy pan, first rinsing the pan in cold water and shaking out the excess before pouring in the milk. (It will help keep the milk from burning in the bottom of the pan.)

Melt the 3 tablespoons of butter in a heavy-bottomed saucepan. Add the flour and let bubble for 3 minutes on low heat to cook the flour. Add the hot milk all at once and whisk vigorously.

Remove from the heat and add salt, pepper, and nutmeg. Add the egg yolk, whisking so the yolk is incorporated smoothly. Set aside. This recipe can be prepared a day ahead of time to this point, then covered with foil and refrigerated.

Clean your copper bowl with salt and vinegar. Rinse and dry it thoroughly (to avoid copper poisoning). Whip the egg whites in it until stiff, fold in all but 2 tablespoons of the grated cheese. Add a small amount of the egg whites to the cream sauce to lighten it. Then reverse the process by pouring the sauce into the egg whites and folding in carefully.

Butter a shallow ovenproof dish of approximately 15 × 9 inches. Spread a small amount of the egg white

3 tablespoons butter
3 tablespoons flour (preferably potato or rice flour)
1 cup milk, scalded
½ teaspoon salt
Freshly ground pepper to taste
½ teaspoon freshly ground nutmeg
1 egg yolk
5 egg whites
Salt to taste
½ cup grated Swiss cheese

mixture onto the bottom. Pile the flaked fish into 6 piles, mounding the egg white mixture on top, and sprinkle each mound with the remaining cheese. (If covered with foil and held for a half hour or less, the recipe can be prepared to this point ahead of time. In this case, make the sauce now, put it in a thermos to hold, and have a drink with your guests. If you have a woodstove, don't worry if the power goes out at this moment.)

Cook in the preheated oven for 15 minutes. The soufflé should be puffed and golden looking, not browned. Serve immediately by cutting around the bottom of each mound with a spatula and lifting it onto individual serving plates. Spoon Sauce Sabayon over the top of each serving.

Sauce Sabayon

3 egg yolks
½ cup whipping cream
¼ cup reduced fish stock
1½ sticks unsalted butter, softened
Salt and freshly ground pepper to taste
Juice of 1 lemon

Place the egg yolks, whipping cream, and fish stock into a heavy-bottomed saucepan. Stirring constantly, let the mixture thicken over low heat. Slowly whip the butter, 1 tablespoon at a time, into the mixture. If it separates because of too much heat or too little whisking, remove from the heat, toss an ice cube into it, and whisk vigorously—it should smooth out. If it does not, place the mixture in a blender or a food processor and run the machine about 10 seconds. Reheat carefully over hot, not boiling, water. Season with salt, pepper, and lemon juice. Serve immediately over the soufflé or hold in a preheated thermos until serving time.

Watercress Salad with Mustard Vinaigrette Dressing

SERVES 6

Wash and dry the watercress. Cut off any big stems. Place in a large salad bowl, and with 2 sharp knives shred the cress into bite-sized pieces. Just before serving, mix and pour dressing sparingly over the greens and toss lightly.

3 large bunches watercress (about 3 cups shredded)
1 cup extra virgin olive oil
⅓ cup cider vinegar
1 tablespoon Aceta Balsamica vinegar
3 tablespoons prepared Dijon mustard
1 hard-boiled egg yolk, mashed
2 cloves of garlic put through a garlic press
¼ teaspoon salt
Freshly ground pepper to taste

Tart Lemon Roulade

SERVES 6 TO 8 AMPLY

LEMON FILLING

Preheat oven to 400°.

Butter a jelly roll pan and line it with parchment paper. Butter the paper lightly. Sprinkle the paper with flour and shake out the excess.

To make the lemon filling, put the water and sugar in a heavy-bottomed saucepan and cook to the soft ball stage (238° on a candy thermometer), or until ½ teaspoon of the mixture forms a soft ball when dropped in cold water.

Beat the egg yolks until they are pale yellow. Pour the hot sugar syrup very slowly into the yolks, beating constantly to prevent the eggs from curdling.

Beat in the vanilla, lemon rind, and lemon juice, and allow to cool. Fold softened butter into the lemon-yolk

½ pound (2 sticks) unsalted butter, softened
5 egg yolks
1½ cups sugar
⅓ cup water
Grated rind of 2 lemons
Juice of 2 lemons
1 teaspoon vanilla extract

mixture and beat until thoroughly mixed. Refrigerate until the sponge cake is complete.

SPONGE CAKE

4 large eggs at room
  temperature
½ teaspoon baking powder
¾ cup sifted flour
⅛ teaspoon salt
½ cup sugar
2 teaspoons grated lemon rind
1 teaspoon lemon juice
3 tablespoons confectioner's
  sugar

To make the sponge cake, preheat oven to 400°.

Have eggs at room temperature. Combine them with the sugar and beat until frothy. Place over warm water (110°) for 15 minutes. Add vanilla. Beat the egg and sugar mixture until it doubles in volume. Sift together the dry ingredients and fold by thirds into the egg and sugar.

Sprinkle the lemon rind over the surface of the mixture, and fold it in. With a rubber spatula gently spread the mixture in the jelly roll pan and bake in the preheated oven for 15 minutes. When a toothpick inserted in the center comes out clean, remove from the oven and let cool for 5 minutes.

Invert the pan onto a tea towel sprinkled with the confectioner's sugar. Peel off the parchment paper and let cool.

Spread the cake with half the lemon filling and, using the towel to exert an even pressure as you go, roll the cake up lengthwise.

Spread the remaining lemon filling mixture smoothly over the outside of the cake, covering any cracks in the surface. Chill for at least 1 hour before serving. If you wish, it can be garnished with very thin lemon slices on top, with a few mint leaves tucked under each slice.

FIFTEEN

A SUPPER TO CELEBRATE SIGNS OF SPRING

May

Cream of Fiddlehead Soup à la D. Davis

◆

Wild Puffballs in Creamy Dill Sauce on Toast

◆

Alsatian Gewurztraminer

◆

Green Salad with Lemony Dressing

◆

Maple Syrup Mousse

In early spring the first woodcocks arrive in Vermont from their winter feeding grounds in the South. There is a place near the Battenkill River where they have been returning year after year to put on a remarkable aerial exhibition that is part of their courtship ritual. It is a cleared meadow, for the singing ground, with some brushy cover and wet bottomland nearby for feeding.

When we quietly walk up to this place at dusk, the male can be heard uttering a cry every few seconds that sounds very much like the electric buzzer on the gate to the safety deposit vault at the local bank. BEEEEEEEP! BEEEEEEEP!

Suddenly, the male takes off on a spiral ascent, twittering as he goes, and widens the circles as he rises perhaps three hundred feet directly above his takeoff site. He then dives for the ground, twisting and zigzagging like a jet-powered leaf. He flutters in for a feather-light landing exactly where he started and begins to buzz again. The whole flight takes about one minute and he repeats it every four or five minutes until he attracts a hen. He certainly claims *our* rapt attention. It's a thrilling manifestation of spring in Vermont.

After a brisk walk back to the house, it's very fitting to have a fireside supper that features other welcome signs of the season: fiddlehead ferns, puffballs, and maple syrup.

Cream of Fiddlehead Soup à la D. Davis

SERVES 6

2 cups fresh fiddleheads, washed to remove brown skins, and drained (Fresh asparagus cut into 1-inch lengths can be substituted for the fiddleheads.)
1 can evaporated milk
1¼ cups chicken stock, or 1¼ cups hot water and 2 chicken bouillon cubes
Pinch of powdered basil, or 1 tablespoon fresh basil leaves, chopped

Place the fiddleheads in a saucepan with the chicken stock or the water and bouillon cubes and bring to a boil. Lower heat and simmer for 8 to 10 minutes, until the fiddleheads are tender when pierced with a fork.

Place the fiddleheads and their liquid in a food processor or blender and purée them. Add the condensed milk and the basil and run the machine for a few seconds to blend. Add salt and pepper to taste.

Warm in a double boiler and serve in heated soup bowls.

Wild Puffballs in Creamy Dill Sauce on Toast

SERVES 6

Cut fairly thick slices of bread and butter them. Place on a cookie sheet and toast in a slow oven at 300° for 12 to 15 minutes. Remove from the oven and set aside on the cookie sheet.

Melt the butter in a large sauté or frying pan, add the oil, and sauté the cubed mushrooms over medium heat for 10 to 12 minutes. Remove to a plate with a slotted spoon and keep warm.

By boiling, reduce the liquid in the pan to approximately ¼ cup. Mix the sour cream, parsley, dill, and lemon juice, and add to the reduced liquid in the pan. Add the mushrooms and mix well.

Place the mushrooms and their sauce over the toast slices on the cookie sheet, sprinkle with the Parmesan cheese and put under the broiler just long enough to melt the cheese and make the sauce start to bubble. Serve immediately.

6 slices Howley White Bread (which see)
2 cups fresh puffballs, cubed into bite-sized pieces (Use fresh oyster mushrooms, chanterelles, or shiitakes in combination with regular domestic mushrooms if you can't find any wild puffballs.)
2 tablespoons butter
2 tablespoons oil
1½ cups sour cream
2 tablespoons fresh parsley, minced
4 tablespoons fresh dill, minced
Juice of 1 lemon
½ cup grated Parmesan cheese

Green Salad with Lemony Dressing

SERVES 6

Use a variety of spring lettuces for the salad and toss them lightly with the simple dressing described here.

Mix the lemon juice and garlic together in a bowl and add the oil slowly, whisking continuously. Whisk in the cream, and add salt and freshly ground pepper to taste. Spoon over the greens and toss lightly just before serving.

1 cup extra virgin olive oil
3 tablespoons lemon juice
2 cloves garlic, put through a garlic press
Salt and pepper to taste
3 tablespoons heavy cream

A Supper to Celebrate Signs of Spring

Maple Syrup Mousse

SERVES 6

1 envelope plus 2 teaspoons
  unflavored gelatin
½ cup cold water
1 cup pure maple syrup
4 egg yolks
½ cup brown sugar
4 egg whites
2 cups heavy cream

Sprinkle the gelatin into the ½ cup cold water and let it soften for about 5 minutes. Then, set the cup in a shallow pan of simmering water and stir until the gelatin has dissolved and is clear. Combine with the maple syrup.

In a large bowl, beat the egg yolks with a whisk until they are light yellow and thickened. Whisk the maple syrup mixture into the yolks and pour it into a small heavy-bottomed saucepan. Cook over medium heat, stirring constantly, until the mixture thickens enough to coat the back of the spoon. Do not let it boil. Remove from the heat, stir in the brown sugar, and mix thoroughly. Transfer to a large bowl and set it aside in a cool place.

Meanwhile, beat the egg whites until stiff. In another bowl whip the cream until it holds its shape softly. With a rubber spatula fold the cream gently but thoroughly into the maple syrup mixture, then add the egg whites, folding until streaks of white no longer show. Rinse a 1½-quart mold in cold water. Shake out the excess water and pour in the mousse mixture. Chill in the refrigerator for at least 4 hours.

To unmold, run a knife around the inside edge of the mold, dip the bottom briefly in hot water, and wipe it dry. Place a chilled serving plate on top of the mold, invert it, and rap it on a table or countertop to loosen the mousse. Chill until ready to serve. The mousse can be garnished with lemon leaves and little maple sugar candies around the bottom, should you want to dress it up.

SIXTEEN

A SPRING LUNCHEON IN HONOR OF A DINOSAUR AND HIS TYPEWRITER

May

Smoked Trout with Lime Mayonnaise

◆

Fiddlehead Ferns and Morel Mushrooms in Vermouth Sauce

◆

Boston Lettuce with French Dressing

◆

Cuvaison Napa Valley Chardonnay

◆

Frozen Grand Marnier Soufflé

Smoked Trout

No trout ever tastes as good as the wild one you caught and cooked on the stream within the hour. We do it so rarely that it's hard to remember how good it is. (We release almost every fish we catch except where it's forbidden, as it is in some trout clubs or on particular rivers abroad.) Running a very close second, however, is smoked trout, warm or cold. If you have to buy your trout frozen or if you fish where the streams are stocked with hatchery fish, this is the best way to get some flavor into them without destroying whatever taste or texture they may possess. It isn't much work if you have one of those little stovetop Swedish smokers that fit right over a burner on top of the stove. Hickory or apple-wood sawdust is spread in the bottom of the pan and the cleaned fish go on the grill for 10 or 12 minutes on each side.

Leave the heads on for this operation. The reason for doing this is to allow you to save the cheeks, the most savory morsel of any fish, located just behind and below the eye. The cheeks will slide out easily with the point of a knife after cooking. Take the pair out and then remove the head and discard it. Place the cheeks (about the size of a small fingernail in a 1½-pound trout) on top of a lemon slice to garnish the trout before you present it. In my opinion this is more appetizing and practical than leaving the whole head on the fish so the guest must remove the cheeks or, worse yet, ignore them.

If you want to serve the trout cold, it will keep a few days in the refrigerator. Being just flavor-smoked it doesn't last long, but you can prepare it a day or two ahead, leaving the skins and heads on until an hour or so before serving.

Trout is very easy to skin after smoking and chilling. With a paring knife, start on an edge of the skin where the fish has been opened, then just peel the skin off and discard it.

Place each fish on an individual serving plate, and garnish with lemon slices and the cheeks of the fish. Surround with French Fried Parsley (*which see*) or fresh watercress, and pass the Lime Mayonnaise in a separate bowl.

POSTSCRIPT: The title refers to a self-styled "dinosaur" fly-fishing writer who insists on being anonymous. He is famously firm in his resolve to *write* words (not process them), on his 41-year-old machine.

Lime Mayonnaise

Place yolks, salt, grated rind and lime juice in a blender or food processor and run for 8 seconds. With the machine running, slowly pour the olive oil into the yolks. It will thicken immediately. Remove to a bowl, grind pepper to taste on top, and serve. (Enough for 6 trout.)

3 egg yolks at room temperature (Place eggs in warm water for 10 minutes if you haven't removed them from the refrigerator in time.)
Grated rind of 2 limes
Juice of 2 limes
½ cup extra virgin olive oil
Salt and freshly ground pepper to taste

Fiddlehead Ferns and Morel Mushrooms in Vermouth Sauce

SERVES 8

2 cups fresh morel mushrooms (Let's hope you are lucky enough to find this many, or are rich enough to buy them. You can use chanterelles, cubed puffballs, or any wild mushroom you recognize instead.)

2 cups fresh fiddlehead ferns (If you are unable to obtain fresh fiddleheads, use asparagus cut into bite-sized pieces instead.)

1 tablespoon oil

5 tablespoons butter

1½ cups heavy cream

¼ cup dry vermouth

Salt and freshly ground white pepper to taste

¾ cup chicken stock (Canned broth is all right.)

6 slices good white bread with crusts removed, toasted and buttered.

Remove stems from the morels and save them for another sauce or soup. With a dampened paper towel wipe any sand or earth off the spongy heads of the mushrooms. (They are very delicate. Do not wash them in running water unless you must.) Slice them in half lengthwise.

Melt the butter and oil in a heavy-bottomed skillet—do not brown. Add the morel halves and sauté them for approximately 5 minutes on each side, depending on their size. They should be just tender and *not* mushy. Add more butter while they are cooking, if necessary, to prevent them from sticking to the pan.

Remove the mushrooms from the pan and keep them warm on a heavy plate on a warming shelf or in an oven turned very low.

Turn the heat up under the skillet, pour in the vermouth, stir to deglaze the pan, and flambé the contents (just touch a long lighted kitchen match to it). Let the flames die down, add the cream, and reduce the heat to low until it is thickened. Add salt and pepper to taste.

Meanwhile, put the fiddleheads into a saucepan, add the chicken stock, and bring to a boil. Lower the heat and simmer for 5 to 7 minutes. They should be crunchy and bright green but not raw tasting.

Drain the fiddleheads well, pat with paper towels to dry further, then add them to the sauce. Add the morels, adjust the seasoning, and arrange the fiddleheads and morels on the toast. Spoon the sauce over them and serve at once.

Boston Lettuce Salad

Wash and dry your Boston lettuce and keep it in a plastic bag in the refrigerator. When ready to serve, arrange it in a salad bowl and toss lightly with the dressing.

FRENCH DRESSING

YIELD-1½ QUARTS

Put all ingredients in a two-quart jar and shake well.

4 teaspoons salt
2 teaspoons onion salt
2 teaspoons white pepper, freshly ground
2 teaspoons dry mustard
1 teaspoon sugar
1 clove garlic, put through a garlic press
2 teaspoons lemon juice
½ teaspoon Worcestershire sauce
12 tablespoons cider vinegar
4 cups extra virgin olive oil

Frozen Grand Marnier Soufflé

7 egg yolks
⅔ cup sugar
1 tablespoon (one packet)
  unflavored gelatin
½ cup water
Juice of ½ lemon
2¼ cups heavy cream
½ cup Grand Marnier

You will need one 3-cup soufflé dish with a paper collar extending at least 4 inches above the top of the dish, and fastened with a rubber band on the outside of the bowl.

Combine the sugar, ¼ cup water, and lemon juice in a saucepan, and boil over medium heat for 3 minutes. Do not let it caramelize or turn brown. Remove from the heat and allow to cool.

Beat the egg yolks until they are light colored and then pour them into the cooled sugar syrup. Beat until thick and fluffy.

Dissolve the gelatin in ¼ cup cold water and then heat gently over low heat, stirring to dissolve. Pour into the yolk-syrup mixture and blend thoroughly.

Beat the cream until thick, add the Grand Marnier, and beat until the mixture is thick and holds a firm shape. Pour the yolk-syrup mixture into the cream mixture and fold gently. Place in the soufflé dish with the collar, smooth the top, and freeze for *at least* 4 hours.

After 4 hours remove the collar. Decorate with whipped cream piped through a pastry tube and candied violets or rose petals, if desired.

Return the soufflé to the freezer until you are ready to serve it. This soufflé will keep well in the freezer for a week if wrapped in plastic wrap and then foil after it is frozen hard.

SEVENTEEN

DINNER WITH THE KING

June

Grilled Whole Atlantic Salmon McConnell with Garlic Mayonnaise

◆

Cucumber-Mint Salad

◆

Boiled Tiny New Potatoes with Dill and Parsley

◆

Watercress Mousse

◆

Moet White Star Extra Dry Champagne

◆

Apricot Whip

◆

Green Pepper Cookies

Grilled Salmon McConnell with Homemade Garlic Mayonnaise

As everyone knows, even a simple hamburger tastes infinitely better if it is grilled out of doors on a charcoal fire. This holds true as well for a fresh Atlantic salmon, truly the king of fish. The flavor is superb. There is a danger that grilling may dry him out excessively, so this recipe uses a homemade mayonnaise that is placed inside the two halves of the fish while grilling. It will keep the inside moist and succulent while the salmon cooks.

You will need a fresh whole Atlantic salmon of any size. (Allow 16 ounces per serving, precooked weight.)

Clean the salmon and leave the skin uncut along the top of the fish so that this skin will hold the fish together. Open the fish flat and spread half the mayonnaise (recipe follows) on the inside of one of the halves. Close the fish and place it on buttered foil large enough to completely envelop it. If you have a hinged wire fish grill, place the wrapped fish in it. (It will be much easier to turn.) If not, place the wrapped fish on a grid over red coals spread so that none are directly below the fish. Cook a 12-pound salmon approximately 20 minutes on each side, turning it just once, very carefully, with two spatulas if you haven't put it in a fish grill.

The internal temperature of the fish when done should be 140° to 150° (insert the Orvis Thermicator right through the foil). If you don't own an Orvis Thermicator, which tells you instantly the internal temperature of anything you are cooking, try Al McClane's method, from *North American Fish Cookery*, of determining doneness in fish:

"Insert the fork into the thickest part of the backbone; the easiest way to do this is to score the fish before cooking with several diagonal cuts spaced about three inches apart (do not score the thin tail section), cutting to, but not through, the backbone. Scoring not only assures more uniform heat penetration but allows an instant reference point for determining protein status . . . A fish is ready for eating at the *instant* protein coagulates when it turns from translucent to opaque.''

Make your diagonal cuts on one side of the fish only. Then you can present it looking intact by flipping the scored side down on the platter.

Remove the fish from the fire, open the foil, and loosen the edges of the skin with the tip of a paring knife. Peel the skin off and discard it. Place the fish on a board or platter and serve it with the reserved half of the mayonnaise alongside.

Place a slice of pimento-stuffed olive over the eye and don't forget to eat the cheeks, just below and behind the eye. In a salmon they can be sizable morsels, and they are always the most delectable part of the fish.

GARLIC MAYONNAISE

Put all ingredients except the oil in a blender, start the machine and pour the oil in *very* slowly. Reserve half in a sauce boat and spread the other half inside the split fish.

1 egg at room temperature
1 teaspoon prepared Dijon mustard
¼ teaspoon garlic salt
Pinch regular salt
2 tablespoons white wine vinegar or plain cider vinegar
1 cup light olive oil (or ¾ cup corn or safflower oil plus ¼ cup olive oil)

Cucumber-Mint Salad

SERVES 8

1 tablespoon lemon juice
¼ cup heavy cream
¼ cup sour cream
3 to 4 medium cucumbers
Salt
1 tablespoon fresh mint leaves, finely minced
1 tablespoon fresh parsley, chopped
Freshly ground pepper

Make the salad dressing at least 2 hours before you plan to use it.

Combine the lemon juice, heavy cream, and sour cream, and let stand 2 hours in refrigerator.

Peel the cucumbers and halve them lengthwise. Remove seeds with a melon baller or scrape a small spoon down the length of the halved cucumber. Slice thinly into a colander. Sprinkle with salt and let stand at least 30 minutes to drain excess liquid. Pat with paper towels to dry and remove excess salt. Combine with cream-lemon mixture and sprinkle with parsley and mint. Grind some pepper over all and chill well.

Boiled Tiny New Potatoes

Allow at least 4 tiny potatoes per person
Butter
1 bunch fresh parsley
1 bunch fresh dill

If you can't get new potatoes, then buy regular sized ones and cut them into quarters or sixths and round off the edges with a potato peeler to a rough oval shape after you have peeled them. If you do have new potatoes, brush well when washing and leave the skins on. Boil until tender, drain, butter generously, add salt and pepper to taste and sprinkle with chopped fresh dill and fresh minced parsley.

Watercress Mousse

SERVES 8

Wash and dry the watercress. Beat the cream cheese until smooth, then mix in the mayonnaise. Dissolve gelatin in chicken stock and cool. Place gelatin mixture and watercress in a blender or food processor and purée. Add Tabasco and mix well, then fold into cheese mixture.

Whip the cream to soft peaks and fold into cheese mixture. Pour into individual custard cups or ramekins and chill until set, about 5 to 6 hours.

When ready to serve, dip the base of the molds into hot water for a few seconds. Turn them out onto serving plates and garnish with a few sprigs of watercress and a halved cherry tomato or a radish rose.

3 bunches watercress (2 cups after puréeing with gelatin and chicken stock)
8 ounces cream cheese, softened
½ cup mayonnaise
1 packet unflavored gelatin
½ cup hot chicken stock (Canned broth is all right.)
Dash Tabasco sauce
½ cup heavy cream

Apricot Whip

SERVES 8

Preheat oven to 325°.

Place the dried apricots with 2 cups water in a small heavy-bottomed saucepan. Bring to a boil and simmer on low heat, covered, for 25 minutes. Reserve 3 tablespoons of the liquid.

Add the orange juice and purée the fruit with the two juices in a food processor or blender, or put through a food mill. Transfer fruit to a mixing bowl.

Beat the egg whites with salt until white and foamy. Add sugar one tablespoon at a time and beat until glossy and stiff.

Fold egg whites into fruit mixture. Spoon into eight 5-ounce custard or soufflé cups, filling them ⅔ full.

Place the cups in a baking pan or dish half filled with boiling water. Bake in preheated oven for 40 minutes. Allow water in pan to cool before removing custard cups. Serve warm or cool, with whipped cream if desired.

1½ cups dried apricots, cooked
3 tablespoons apricot juice
3 tablespoons orange juice
3 large egg whites at room temperature
¼ teaspoon salt
½ cup sugar
½ pint whipping cream (optional)
3 tablespoons confectioner's sugar (optional)

This is an old-fashioned dessert that isn't used enough now. It can be made with an equal amount of any dried fruit: apples, pears, peaches, prunes, or a combination of dried fruits. It's light, refreshing, easily digested and doesn't require much skill or time to prepare. If you use a sugar substitute and omit the whipped cream it can also be low in calories while still retaining its delicious flavor.

Green Pepper Cookies

MAKES 5 DOZEN

5 cups sifted flour
1 teaspoon baking soda
1¼ teaspoons cinnamon
1¼ teaspoons ginger
1 teaspoon ground cloves
½ teaspoon ground dry green
    peppercorns
1 cup (2 sticks) butter, softened
1 cup dark corn syrup
1 cup sugar
1 tablespoon cider vinegar
2 eggs, beaten

This recipe requires *dry* green peppercorns, *not* the ones that are canned in vinegar or oil. They can be hard to find, but most specialty and gourmet food stores carry them. The dough must be refrigerated for 3 hours before baking.

Sift together the first 6 ingredients. Combine the butter, syrup, and vinegar in a saucepan and heat until butter melts. Cool and stir into dry ingredients and beaten eggs, mixing well. Cover with plastic wrap or foil and refrigerate for 3 hours.

Preheat oven to 350°.

Divide the dough into 4 portions and remove only 1 at a time from the refrigerator. Roll to ⅛-inch thickness on a lightly floured board. Cut into desired shapes. (A fish would be very fitting for this meal.) Place ¾ inch apart on a lightly greased cookie sheet and bake 7 to 8 minutes. Transfer to a wire rack or waxed paper to cool.

After cooling, store in a covered tin container to retain the great crispness. They go with simple diced fresh fruit or with ice cream as well as with apricot whip.

Serve your favorite champagne with this meal. The king of fish, the Atlantic salmon, deserves this accompaniment. So do you, especially if you caught him.

EIGHTEEN

A FAST AND EASY LUNCHEON FOR DEPARTING HOUSE GUESTS

June

ROQUEFORT SOUFFLÉ

◆

MIXED GREEN SALAD WITH FRENCH DRESSING

◆

CRUSTY FRENCH BREAD

◆

GRAPEFRUIT MELBA

This is a very easy, quickly made luncheon, but it is not just fast food. The soufflé is rich, velvety, and flavorful. The dessert is tart and tangy. They are both unusual in flavor and ease of preparation.

Roquefort Soufflé

SERVES 6

6 eggs, separated
1 teaspoon Worcestershire
  sauce
1½ cups Roquefort cheese (or 1
  cup Roquefort and ½ cup
  Gruyère)
11 ounces cream cheese
½ cup whipping cream
Salt and freshly ground white
  pepper

Preheat oven to 375°.

Put everything except the egg whites and the cheeses in a food processor. Run for 10 seconds. Crumble in the Roquefort and add the cream cheese and whipping cream. Run for another 10 seconds.

Butter a 1½-quart soufflé dish. Beat the egg whites until stiff. Fold a small amount of the egg whites into the cheese mixture to lighten it, then reverse the process and pour the cheese mixture into the egg whites and fold in carefully.

Bake for 20 to 30 minutes, or until lightly browned and puffed. Serve immediately.

When served, the center should be soft and runny, the outside edge firm. A true soufflé never needs a sauce if it is baked properly. The outside, firm part should be served first and then some of the more liquid center spooned over it.

Use an assortment of greens for your salad and use the French Dressing recipe (which see). If you can't buy good French bread in your neighborhood, use crusty, hard French-style rolls that come in a package.

The dessert is even easier to make than the soufflé.

Grapefruit Melba

1 pink grapefruit for each 2
  people
½ cup red currant jelly for each
  whole grapefruit
½ cup seedless red raspberry
  jelly for each whole grapefruit
Orange sherbet (1 scoop per
  person)

Cut the grapefruit in half and loosen the sections with a grapefruit knife. Place a scoop of orange sherbet on top of each grapefruit half and top with the raspberry and currant jelly mixture, which has been melted over low heat.

This is a refreshing and colorful dessert. Even a child can do it. In fact, I do remember doing it as a child.

NINETEEN

A RIVERSIDE REPAST
FOLLOWING THE EVENING RISE

July

BAGNA CAUDA WITH CRUDITÉS

◆

GRILLED SIRLOIN STEAK

◆

LES OEUFS "À LA TRIPE"

◆

GARLIC ITALIAN BREAD

◆

OAK LEAF LETTUCE WITH FRESH BASIL DRESSING

◆

BURGESS NAPA VALLEY CABERNET SAUVIGNON

◆

SHORTCAKE WITH BLUEBERRIES AND CREAM

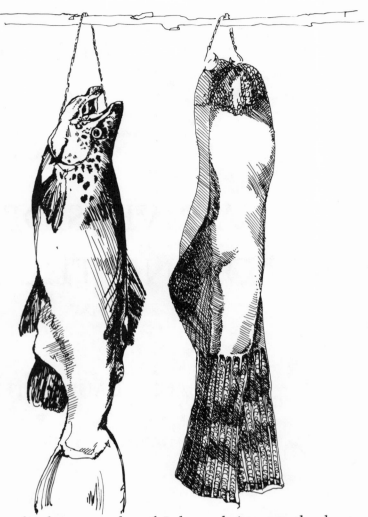

During the hot months of July and August the best time of the day to fish is between seven-thirty and nine in the evening. Guests arrive in hip boots or waders and fish the evening rise of brook and brown trout before dinner. Of course, we don't keep the fish to eat. We have charcoal grilled steak and put the fish back to catch again another day. (Some have been caught three times in a season.)

Over the years Leigh and the boys traditionally have grilled a steak on the riverbank and made sandwiches from it as they hunkered in front of the fire. It is so pleasant by the water at dusk. The little riffle splashes. The fireflies come out and flash on and off. The moon rises over the Green Mountains.

When entertaining visiting fishermen from as far away as Japan or New Zealand, the setting remains as beautiful as before, but the menu and presentation become a trifle more chic. One cannot help feeling that it is a little too casual to have guests come halfway around the world to sit on a muddy bank and choke down a piece of steak between two slabs of bread.

It took some time to get the operation running smoothly. I remember the first such outing clearly. The table was placed near the riffle complete with cloth, centerpiece, and candles. A complete bar was set up. A hot casserole, salad, and dessert augmented the menu. It seemed a long way from eating a simple steak sandwich while huddled around a little campfire. That is, until I asked our youngest son, then fourteen, who had just crawled up the bank from fishing, to get some water to put out a flareup under the steak. He had just removed one leg of his waders (which leaked, of course). Being the obedient son he always has been, he immediately whipped off his dripping sock and wrung it out over the steak. The Japanese guests discreetly watched the moon rise.

Before setting off up or down the riverbank, everyone has a drink and a fairly substantial hors d'oeuvre to keep from starving before nine or nine-thirty. One of the favorite predinner choices is Bagna Cauda. The Orvis dealer from Turin passed judgment on this version and pronounced it the best he'd had outside the Piedmont region of Italy. It consists of a heated sauce into which icy cold vegetables are dipped and then eaten. If desired, a more filling snack can be made out of it with cubed French or Italian bread or breadsticks taking the place of the vegetables.

Bagna Cauda with Crudités

SERVES 12

Wash, prepare as directed, and chill in individual plastic bags.

2 green bell peppers, cut into ½-inch strips
2 red bell peppers, cut into ½-inch strips
2 bunches small scallions
2 cups broccoli flowerets
8 stalks celery, julienned
2 cups cauliflower, in bite-sized pieces

SAUCE

16 flat canned anchovy fillets,
   mashed with a fork
4 large cloves of garlic, put
   through a garlic press
4 cups heavy cream
¼ pound unsalted butter
8 or 10 grinds pepper
Optional but desirable: 1 white
   truffle, finely minced

Reduce the cream to 2 cups by boiling in a very heavy-bottomed saucepan over moderately high heat. Stir occasionally until it begins to thicken, then lower the heat and stir continuously until it measures 2 cups. Pour into a small bowl and set aside.

In a small heavy frying pan, melt the 4 tablespoons of butter over low heat. Add the garlic and anchovies. Do not allow to brown. Stir in the reduced cream, the pepper, and the minced truffle. Do not let it boil.

Serve in a small pottery bowl over a candle warmer. It usually disappears so quickly that you won't have to worry over how to keep it warm for a long period.

Arrange the chilled vegetables on a platter, keeping them in separate groups so the colors will have more impact. Place them next to the sauce with a generous supply of paper napkins, or fondue forks if you are using the cubed bread.

Everyone has his favorite way to grill a steak. This time buy a nice sirloin 3 inches thick. It will serve 10 to 12. If you're having fewer people, buy a porterhouse steak—it will serve half that many. It takes about 20 minutes on each side to cook, so start the fire early. Ideally, the internal temperature should be 120° to 130°. Slice thinly for serving.

Oeufs "à la Tripe"

SERVES 10 TO 12

Don't worry, there is no tripe in this dish. It is a combination of sautéed onions and hard-boiled eggs. If this sounds even worse than tripe, keep an open mind and try it. It's perfect with a grilled steak or any red meat. It acquired its name because the method of cooking the onions is the same as that used to cook tripe. It's also a really wonderful way to use up all those hard-boiled eggs following the annual visit of the Easter Bunny.

Peel and slice the eggs and set aside. Melt 8 tablespoons of butter with the oil in a large heavy-bottomed skillet and add the sliced onions and ¼ teaspoon salt. Cover and cook over low heat, stirring occasionally, for 20 to 30 minutes. The onions should be soft and golden, but not browned.

Scald the milk, first rinsing the pan in cold water and shaking out the excess. Sprinkle the potato flour over the onions and stir it in while cooking for 3 minutes. Remove the onions from the heat and pour the scalding milk over them. Stir until the sauce is smooth, return to low heat, and simmer for 3 minutes to cook the flour completely.

Add the cream very gradually and stir until smooth. Season with salt and pepper to taste and grate the whole nutmeg over the top. Stir again to combine thoroughly and remove from the heat.

Spread half the onion mixture in the bottom of a shallow ovenproof baking dish. Cover with half of the sliced eggs in a layer. Repeat with another onion layer and, finally, the remaining half of the sliced eggs.

Sprinkle on the grated Swiss cheese, dot with butter, and place in the preheated oven for 2 or 3 minutes, until the cheese has melted and the top is golden brown.

Remove from the oven, and put foil over the top. Line a large basket with several layers of Turkish towels, lower the casserole into it and cover with more towels. It will keep warm this way in a draft-free place for 1 to 2 hours, or until the evening hatch is over.

14 hard-boiled eggs, peeled and
 sliced about ⅓ inch thick
8 tablespoons butter
3 tablespoons oil
6 medium-sized yellow onions
 (3½ cups sliced)
Salt to taste
6 tablespoons flour (potato or
 rice flour is preferable)
2½ cups milk
Freshly ground black pepper
1 whole nutmeg
¾ cup heavy cream
⅓ cup imported Swiss cheese
2 tablespoons butter

Oak Leaf Lettuce with Fresh Basil Dressing

SERVES 6

For the salad, use Boston lettuce if you can't find oak leaf. It should be a soft, buttery type. Wash and dry it and chill in plastic bags that can go right into the cooler of ice you're taking along on the picnic. Pack some serving tongs and a big salad bowl and take the dressing along in a jar.

FRESH BASIL SALAD DRESSING

½ cup fresh basil leaves, firmly
  packed
1 tablespoon fresh parsley,
  finely minced
1 tablespoon tarragon vinegar
4 tablespoons soy oil
½ teaspoon salt
Freshly ground green pepper

Finely mince the basil leaves by using the on-off technique with your food processor, or chop them by hand. Put them and all the other ingredients into a pint jar, screw the lid on firmly, and shake. This has a beautiful green color and makes an aromatic, palate-cleansing salad to go with the steak and the Oeufs "à la Tripe."

Shortcake with Blueberries and Cream

SERVES 6

2 cups flour
3 tablespoons sugar
1 stick cold butter, cut into 8
  pieces
1 teaspoon baking powder
¼ cup cold heavy cream
2 pints blueberries, washed and
  drained well
2 tablespoons confectioner's
  sugar
Real whipped cream (in a spray
  can for convenience)

Preheat oven to 375°.

Place flour, sugar, and baking powder in a food processor or sift into a bowl. With the processor running, drop the butter by pats into the feed tube. Add the cream and mix just until moistened. (Cut the butter in by hand if you don't have a food processor, add the cream, and mix lightly.) Pat the dough down into the baking dish until level and bake in the preheated oven for 20 to 25 minutes, until golden in color. (If you want to double this recipe, bake the shortcake in 2 separate pie plates or 1 large shallow baking dish.)

Sprinkle the confectioner's sugar on the berries and pack in a plastic bag. Pack the canned whipped cream in the ice chest, wrap the shortcake in foil in its baking dish, pack in a basket, and you're ready for a lovely evening on the river after you load all those baskets and coolers into the station wagon. Don't forget to pack the wineglasses and the corkscrew.

TWENTY

A DINNER THAT RECALLS NORMANDY

July

VEAL SWEETBREADS IN VERMOUTH-CREAM SAUCE

◆

BUTTERED LONG GRAIN RICE

◆

BRAISED LEEKS, SWEET RED PEPPERS, AND CARROTS

◆

ROSÉ DE PROVENCE

◆

CALVADOS APPLE TART

Fly fishing on the chalk streams of France and England is a delight in July. The River Risle runs right through the middle of the small village of La Riviere Thibouville in Normandy, much as the Test River runs right through the village of Stockbridge in Hampshire.

On the Risle the rises occur from 7:00 P.M. on through the evening until dark, so there is plenty of time for sightseeing during the day. Nearby is Monet's home in Giverny, and Mont St. Michel is a comfortable morning's drive away.

Two ingredients that recall Normandy most vividly are Calvados, the apple liqueur made in the region, and heavy cream. They are used in the main dish and the dessert here. Of course, there is a tremendous variety of food available. The stalls in the market at Rouen are loaded with every imaginable fruit and vegetable, fish and fowl.

Perhaps because one is fishing, there is a tendency to want to eat something other than fish. Veal sweetbreads were featured on the menu at the Hotel Soleil d'Or one evening and even though it isn't finny, this dish recalls an extremely pleasant angling vacation.

GAME IN SEASON

Veal Sweetbreads in Vermouth-Cream Sauce

SERVES 6

Before cooking the sweetbreads, make certain that you have allowed them to soak under cold, running water for at least 1 hour to thoroughly cleanse them —3 or 4 hours is even better. Don't be discouraged by the apparent fussing that is necessary to prepare this. It is really worth it.

As much as 3 days in advance, place the sweetbreads in a pan with the vegetables and water to cover them and bring to the boiling point. Turn the heat off under the pan and let cool. If you're preparing them for that day, continue. If not, refrigerate the sweetbreads in their liquid until the day you want to serve them.

When ready to use the sweetbreads, remove the thin membrane from the outside with a sharp paring knife. Cut lengthwise in half, salt and pepper them, lightly dredge in flour, and set aside.

Sauté the chopped shallots and sliced mushrooms in separate pans until they are soft, not browned. Heat a large frying pan, melt 8 tablespoons of butter with the oil, and add the sweetbread halves. Sauté them on each side until they are golden brown, lower the heat, and cook for 7 or 8 minutes. Add the shallots and mushrooms. Heat the vermouth in a small pan, pour it over the sweetbreads, and light it with a long kitchen match. When the flames have died down, add the cream and simmer on low heat until only heated through. Add salt and pepper to taste. Remove to a heated serving dish and sprinkle the top with the minced parsley. Serve immediately.

Meanwhile, cook your favorite long grain rice according to package instructions and butter, salt, and pepper it to taste. The sweetbread dish needs a plain white rice, not wild rice. Serve the rice beneath the sweetbreads and their sauce.

6 pairs (1 per person) veal sweetbreads
2 carrots, chopped roughly
Top half of 3 celery stalks, including leaves
3 sprigs each of parsley and tarragon
3 bay leaves
8 peppercorns

SAUCE

2 medium onions, sliced
½ cup vermouth
4 cups cream: 2 heavy, 2 half-and-half
½ cup chopped shallots
1 cup sliced mushrooms
Salt and pepper
¼ cup flour
8 tablespoons butter and 1 tablespoon oil
¼ cup minced fresh parsley

Braised Leeks, Red Peppers, and Carrots

SERVES 6 AMPLY

3 large leeks
8 carrots
2 large sweet red peppers
3 tablespoons olive oil
2 tablespoons butter
½ cup chicken stock (Canned broth is all right.)
Salt and freshly ground black pepper

Preheat oven to 325°.

Wash the leeks and cut off tops, leave 1 inch of the green part. Cut in half lengthwise and rinse again under cold running water, fanning the leaves with your thumb from each side of the leek. Make sure you wash out all the grit, keeping the halves intact. Place cut side down on paper towels to drain. Julienne finely in a food processor or by hand.

Wash the peppers, and core and julienne them. Dry with paper towels. Clean carrots with a potato peeler, and dry and julienne them. Keep the three vegetables separate and stacked in the same direction. They will make a bigger impact visually if the colors are in separate blocks in the serving dish. They require different cooking times also.

Melt the butter in the oil in a large sauté pan. Place the carrots in carefully, keeping the strips all going in the same direction. Try not to crowd them in the pan. Cook the carrots for 7 minutes, turning once with a spatula. Do not brown them. Remove to a shallow ovenproof baking dish, placing them at one end, stacked neatly and covering a third of the space. Sauté the leeks for 4 minutes, adding a little more oil and butter if necessary. Remove them to the baking dish next to the carrots.

Lastly, sauté the julienned peppers for 3 minutes and add to the last third of the baking dish. Pour over all the ½ cup of chicken stock and place in the preheated oven for 15 minutes. They will hold in a warm oven for 20 to 30 minutes, if necessary. Cover with foil if they seem to be drying out.

Calvados Apple Tart

SERVES 6 TO 8

PIE CRUST (PÂTÉ BRISÉE)

Preheat oven to 400°.

Sift flour, sugar, and salt into a food processor and run 6 seconds. Through the feed tube add the yolk and water and run machine until a ball of dough forms. Remove, wrap in plastic wrap, and allow dough to rest for 15 minutes in the refrigerator.

If preparing by hand, cut the butter into the sifted dry ingredients, add the water and yolk, and mix just enough to moisten. Wrap and allow to rest in refrigerator as above.

Roll out the dough on a floured board to a ⅛-inch thickness. Use a 10- or 11-inch quiche dish or a flan pan with a removable bottom. Prick the bottom and sides of the dough with a fork. Put a sheet of foil over the unbaked crust and place pie weights or uncooked beans or rice on top of the foil. Bake in the preheated oven for 10 minutes. Remove the foil and weights and bake 2 to 4 minutes more until lightly golden in color. Remove from the heat and cool.

2 cups flour
1 scant teaspoon sugar
1 teaspoon salt
¾ cup (1½ sticks) unsalted butter, sliced into pats
1 egg yolk
4 to 6 tablespoons ice water

GLAZE

Melt a 12-ounce jar of apricot jam, strain through a sieve, and add 2 tablespoons Calvados.

Brush the cooled tart shell with some of the glaze, reserving the remainder for later.

CRÈME FRAÎCHE

Mix together 1 cup commercial sour cream and 2 cups heavy cream. Let stand at room temperature 5 to 6 hours.

FILLING

7 to 8 Granny Smith apples
½ cup (1 stick) unsalted butter
⅓ cup sugar
Peel of ½ lemon, grated
¼ cup Calvados
½ cup heavy cream
⅓ cup sugar
½ teaspoon cinnamon
1 egg
2 teaspoons vanilla
¼ teaspoon freshly grated
   nutmeg

Reset oven to 375°.

To prepare the filling, peel and core 6 of the apples. Cut them into sixths. Melt butter in a large heavy skillet over a medium heat. Add the apples, sugar, and lemon peel, and sauté until apples are slightly caramelized. Blend in ¼ cup Calvados, and cook 1 or 2 minutes. Remove apples with a slotted spoon and reduce the liquid to 2 tablespoons by boiling.

Heat together the ½ cup heavy cream, sugar, cinnamon, and ¼ teaspoon freshly grated nutmeg to scalding. Lightly beat the egg in a bowl and gradually add the cream mixture, whisking constantly so the egg doesn't curdle. Add the vanilla and the reduced liquid from the apples.

Spread the sautéed apples in the pie shell. Halve the remaining 1 or 2 apples, peel, core, and cut into paper-thin slices. Arrange in a fan pattern over the cooked apples. Pour the custard mixture over the apples to within ⅛ inch of the top.

Position the baking rack to the lower third of the oven and bake 30 to 40 minutes, until top apples are tender. Remove from oven. Heat the broiler. If using a flan pan, remove the outer ring. Sprinkle the 2 or 3 tablespoons of sugar on top of the tart. Broil 6 to 8 inches from the heat until the top is caramelized. Watch it carefully, you don't want to scorch it now. You're almost through making the best apple pie you ever tasted.

GARNISH

2 to 3 tablespoons sugar
¼ cup chopped toasted
   pistachios or almonds
Crème fraîche

Remove from the heat and cool. Brush the surface with the remainder of the apricot glaze and sprinkle the nuts on top. Serve at room temperature with the crème fraîche spooned over it.

No one will ask you what you have been doing all day when they taste this. If someone does, it's a justifiable homicide.

TWENTY-ONE

A SUPREME SALMON LUNCHEON

July

GRAVLAX WITH TRADITIONAL ICELANDIC DILL SAUCE

◆

RYE BRITTLE BREAD

◆

CLOS DU VAL NAPA VALLEY CHARDONNAY

◆

CUCUMBER AND PEPPER SALAD

◆

BLUEBERRY-ALMOND CRISP

In the latter part of July or the first part of August one suddenly wonders why on earth he left the sunny slopes of Vermont or the balmy afternoons in Nantucket to go stand in the sleet in a freezing river in Iceland. There isn't even a tree or rock big enough to stand behind or crawl under to avoid the wind. But, one eventually thinks of gravlax on pumpernickel with dill sauce and, with renewed vigor, makes eighty more casts into the howling wind. When one feels that authoritative tug on the line, it's all worth any temporary discomfort and the several thousand dollars spent getting there. One has caught the king of fish, an Atlantic salmon.

It doesn't sleet every day. Once the temperature rose to sixty-eight degrees and the sun shone brilliantly. All the guides immediately took their shirts off and the cook fainted in the kitchen from the excessive heat. It was so bright that the salmon lay on the bottom like logs and wouldn't go near any fly that dangled tantalizingly near. After we had tried fifty different patterns, Leigh tied on a Hornburg and used it dry, skittering it across the slick water. Wham! A salmon leaped half out of the water to get it. The guides had *never* seen anything like it: a salmon taking a *dry* fly. They continued to stare in amazement as four of us, one after the other, took a nice salmon with the same method. So much for taking a guide's advice as gospel.

Another thing the guide might balk at is your refusal to let all the fish go to the smokehouse. Clean one or two right there on the river and make gravlax. It can be frozen and used up to nine months later for an unforgettable first course or meal.

Gravlax, without doubt, is the purist's favorite way to eat Atlantic salmon. It dramatically demonstrates the superior quality of this most-prized fish. The flavor is more delicate than smoked. It has a firm, satiny texture and a beautiful pale color.

It must be made 2 days before it is to be served. The salt, pepper and herbs cure it, and this cannot be rushed.

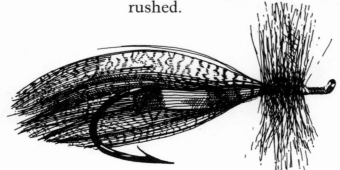

Gravlax

An 8-pound salmon is ideal for this dish. Fillet the fish, in half, leaving the skin on. Lay the two fillets flat on a counter or board, skin side down. Then take out the twenty-odd rib bones that have been unavoidably severed when you filleted the salmon. Use your index finger to locate the brittle ends of bone (about 1 inch below the fish's back), and pull them *slowly* out with a clean pair of pliers.

Mix the dill weed, pepper, and salt together (you can pack this in a plastic bag or jar and take it wherever you go fishing). Spread the spices evenly over the fillet halves.

Spread brown sugar ¼ inch thick on one fillet, and sandwich the halves together. Slide the fish into a large plastic bag, and remove air from the bag by rolling it up. Fold the end over and tape it securely shut—it has to be airtight. (A good way is to start at the opposite end from the open one and wrap tape around and around the fish as you roll up the bag, finally taping the open end shut where it is doubled over on itself.) This whole process takes less than 20 minutes.

Put the packaged fish between 2 boards or trays and weight it down with 5 or 6 pounds of canned goods, books, rocks, or old flatirons. If the temperature is 70° or lower, leave it out for 24 hours, turning it over every 8 hours during that period. If the temperature is over 70°, refrigerate the salmon (with weights) for 48 hours. Refrigerate for at least 4 hours before serving if you have cured it at room temperature.

To serve, unwrap the fish and scrape away most of the dill and spices and pat dry with a paper towel. Slice thinly with a very sharp knife *on the diagonal*.

For a luncheon, arrange 3 or 4 slices on buttered pumpernickel bread, garnish with one or 2 paper-thin slices of sweet onion, a few capers, and serve with the traditional Icelandic mustard-dill sauce.

A smaller portion makes a lovely first course for a seated dinner party. For canapés, use the gravlax plain and thinly sliced, accompanied with a tray of freshly baked Rye Brittle Bread.

1 fresh salmon, any size
¼ cup medium-ground pepper (An easy equivalent is one 2-ounce jar of Java black pepper, medium grind.)
¼ cup dried dill (One 2-ounce jar dillweed)
1 pound light brown sugar
1 cup salt
A plastic bag large enough to hold the size salmon you aspire to catch
Packaging tape
5 pounds of weight (canned goods, books, old flatirons)
1 clean pair of pliers

Traditional Icelandic Dill Sauce

SERVES 8

1 cup light olive oil or cooking
 oil
4 tablespoons cider vinegar
2 tablespoons Swedish mustard
 (Dijon is fine, too.)
1 tablespoon sugar
2 tablespoons minced fresh dill

Whisk first 4 ingredients together, add the dill, mix lightly, and serve in a sauce boat next to the gravlax.

Rye Brittle Bread

YIELD: 4 FLAT SHEETS

1 package dry yeast
1 cup warm water
¼ pound (1 stick) unsalted
 butter, melted, plus ½ stick
 butter melted separately
1½ teaspoons salt
1 teaspoon sugar
1 cup white all-purpose flour
3 cups rye flour
2 tablespoons caraway seeds
 (optional)

Pour warm water into a large bowl, sprinkle in the yeast and stir until thoroughly dissolved. Add sugar, salt, and ¼ pound melted butter, and whisk until sugar and salt are dissolved. Add 2 cups rye flour and beat until smooth.

Sift together 1 cup rye flour and 1 cup white flour and add to the first mixture to make a stiff dough. Divide into 2 batches and run each in a food processor with a steel blade for 3 minutes. If dough is too dry, add 2 tablespoons water, one at a time, watching for the dough to form into a ball. Or knead for 8 to 10 minutes by hand.

Form into one large ball and place in a buttered bowl, rolling to coat with butter. Cover with a clean tea towel and let rise in a warm place until doubled in bulk, about 1 hour.

Preheat oven to 350° if you want to bake it now.

Punch the dough down and divide into 4 equal pieces. Take one piece at a time and pat together in a small rectangle on a lightly floured piece of waxed paper. (Wipe the counter with a damp sponge before placing the waxed paper so that it will stay in place.) Roll out into a rough rectangle of about 12 × 14 inches. It should be as thin as possible.

This is a very elastic dough and if you have trouble rolling it out. Push the rolling pin away from your body, not back and forth. Lift the dough and turn it on the paper in order to roll it out evenly.

At this point, you can proceed to bake the bread or hold it until you want to use it. It is much better fresh and piping hot from the oven. To keep, simply roll up the wax paper with the dough inside it, wrap it in foil, and refrigerate for up to 6 hours until you want to bake it. Or wrap and freeze for months. Take it out of the freezer at least 3 hours before you want to bake it, so it has time to defrost completely before you try to unroll it.

To bake, place the unrolled rectangle on an ungreased cookie sheet in the preheated oven for 8 minutes. Melt the ½ stick of butter. Remove the bread from the oven, brush melted butter over the entire surface, and sprinkle on the caraway seeds. Return to the oven quickly and bake about 5 to 6 minutes more. It should be lightly browned and crisp. Slide whole on a silver platter or a board and allow guests to break off individual servings.

Cucumber and Pepper Salad

SERVES 8

Peel and seed cucumbers (a melon baller works well to seed). Cut into 2-inch lengths. In a large bowl, stir the lime juice and salt together until the salt dissolves. Drop in the cucumbers and peppers, mix thoroughly, and cover with foil or plastic wrap. Marinate at room temperature for at least 8 hours before serving.

3 medium-sized cucumbers
2 tablespoons fresh lime juice
1¼ teaspoons salt
3 green bell peppers, cut into 2-inch squares

Blueberry-Almond Crisp

2 pints fresh blueberries
½ cup sugar
½ teaspoon nutmeg, freshly grated
Juice of 1 lemon
¼ pound butter
1 cup flour
1 cup blanched almonds, ground
⅔ cup sugar
1 teaspoon vanilla extract

Preheat oven to 400°.

Wash blueberries, drain, and place in an enamel pan. Add sugar and lemon juice and let stand 1 hour.

Grind almonds in food processor or blender. Add flour, sugar, and vanilla and run the machine a few seconds to mix well. With the machine running drop in butter, 1 tablespoon at a time, through the feed tube and process 5 seconds. (If doing this by hand, cut butter into the mixture of dry ingredients and mix well.) Remove to a bowl and set aside in a cool place.

Put blueberries, sugar, and lemon juice on low heat, bring to a boil, and simmer gently 10 to 12 minutes. Don't let the berries turn to mush. Remove from heat and add nutmeg. Sieve the juice off the berries into a heavy-bottomed pan. Place juice on the heat and reduce it to a thick syrup, about 15 minutes. Stir frequently and keep the heat low so the juice barely bubbles.

Butter an ovenproof dish, approximately 9 × 12 × 2 inches. Pour blueberries into a dish and pour the heavy syrup over them. Take half the almond-flour mixture and sprinkle over the top of the berries. Place in the preheated oven for 10 minutes.

Remove from the oven and sprinkle the remaining half of the almond mixture on top. Replace in the oven for another 8 to 10 minutes, until the top is lightly browned. Remove from the oven and let cool at least 15 minutes before serving. Serve warm or at room temperature.

TWENTY-TWO

COLD DUCK ON A HOT SUMMER DAY

August

COLD DUCK SALAD TAMARI

◆

SPRING MOUNTAIN NAPA VALLEY CABERNET SAUVIGNON

◆

STRAWBERRIES MARGARITA

Somehow, the prospect of eating a duck dinner in the summer is unappealing. However, this is the time to clean out the freezer and make room for pesto sauce and other products from the garden. (If I don't have thirty quarts of pesto frozen by the end of August, I start feeling insecure.)

There are usually a few overlooked frozen ducks in a corner of the freezer and I cook them early in the morning before the heat of day, chill them, and make duck salad. This is also a good way to use leftover duck any time of the year, especially when the house-guest situation calls for more than a simple duck sandwich. The presentation looks elegant, and the combination of crisp rice noodles and lettuce with the chilled duck and sauce tastes elegant too. This can be made with domestic duck very successfully.

Cold Duck Salad Tamari

SERVES 4

2 medium-sized wild ducks, or
   2 Long Island ducklings
4 scallions, green part only
3 to 4 ounces rice sticks
½ head Boston lettuce
¼ cup tamari soy sauce
1 tablespoon rice vinegar
1 clove garlic, put through a
   garlic press
½ teaspoon prepared Dijon
   mustard
¼ teaspoon powdered ginger
6 large fresh mushrooms
½ lemon

Preheat oven to 450°.

The day before, or early in the morning of the day of serving, put the ducks breast up in a shallow baking pan with a splash of water. Bake in a 450° oven for 10 to 12 minutes. (Long Island duckling is larger and may take a little longer.) The internal temperature when done should be 140°. Remove from the oven and cool. The breasts can be filleted from the birds and chilled in the refrigerator—it will be easier to julienne them when you are ready to assemble the salad. Make Duck Soup (*which see*) or duck stock from the remainder of the birds.

While the ducks are cooking, prepare the rice noodles by deep frying in small batches in safflower oil. Heat the oil to smoking hot and drop a few noodles in at a time. They will puff up immediately and curl. Do not brown them, they should be golden in color. Remove to paper towels to drain, and when cool store in a covered tin or tightly sealed plastic bag to preserve crispness.

Finely julienne the green scallion tops and refrigerate in a plastic bag. Slice the mushrooms thinly and squeeze the lemon juice over them. Chill in the refrigerator. Stack the washed and dried lettuce leaves 4 or 5 at a time, roll up like a cigar, and slice very thin. Chill in a plastic bag in the refrigerator.

Combine the tamari sauce, vinegar, garlic, mustard, and ginger, and whisk thoroughly. Cover and chill in the refrigerator.

Skin and julienne the duck breasts into thin strips. Return to the refrigerator in a plastic bag.

When ready to serve, place the crisp noodles on 4 plates. Cover the noodles lightly with the finely shredded lettuce. Sprinkle all but 4 of the mushroom slices and most of the scallions over the lettuce, reserving the rest for garnish.

Arrange the julienned duck on top and pour 2 or 3 tablespoons of the tamari mixture over each salad. Garnish each salad with the reserved strips of green scallion and a mushroom slice and serve immediately. A crusty bread and sweet butter go well with this.

Cold Duck on a Hot Summer Day

Strawberries Margarita

SERVES 4

1 quart fresh strawberries
2 cups sour cream
3 tablespoons light, dry tequila
¼ teaspoon cinnamon
2 tablespoons finely grated lime rind
1 tablespoon finely grated orange rind
3 tablespoons coarsely ground almonds
Lime wedges (garnish)

Hull, wash, and drain the strawberries on paper towels. Cut them in half and chill in the refrigerator. Whisk together the remaining ingredients and chill.

When ready to serve, place the strawberries in a clear crystal or glass bowl or individual footed serving dishes. Spoon the tequila sauce over them and garnish with a wedge of lime for each serving.

TWENTY-THREE

A DINNER PRECEDING
THE SUMMER THEATRE

August

SMOKED SALMON WITH GINGER MAYONNAISE

◆

STEAMED TINY NEW POTATOES

◆

FRESH HARICOTS VERTS

◆

TOMATO AND DILL SALAD

◆

POUILLY FUMÉ

◆

COINTREAU SPONGE WITH BLUEBERRIES AND PEACHES

Smoked Salmon with Ginger Mayonnaise

SAUCE

6 egg yolks
Juice of 4 limes
Grated rind of 2 limes
1 cup light olive oil
1 cup peeled and diced fresh
   ginger
Salt and pepper to taste
4 tablespoons sugar
1 cup water
White wine as thinner
8 whole fresh basil leaves for
   garnish

8 large slices smoked salmon
   (sliced with the grain, not
   down across it), each slice
   about 4 × 6 inches
2 cups julienned scallions
2 cups julienned cucumber,
   peeled and seeded
2 cups julienned basil leaves
   (fresh)
Freshly ground green
   peppercorns

SERVES 8

Combine ginger, sugar, and water in a heavy saucepan. Simmer until ginger is tender, about 15 minutes. Purée in a food processor and strain into small bowl. Set aside.

Combine yolks, salt, and lime juice in mixer, on high speed. Slowly add the oil in a steady stream. Season with salt and freshly ground pepper. Add ginger purée and lime rind. Thin to light sauce consistency with dry white wine, if necessary.

If you are using smoked salmon that you have frozen, slice it as soon as a knife will penetrate it. It's much easier to get thin, neat slices while it's still partially frozen, rather than after it has thawed completely. Be sure to slice with the grain, not straight down.

Lay the slices of smoked salmon flat. Spread scallions, basil, and cucumber evenly on the salmon. Grind the green peppercorns to taste over all. Roll salmon up tightly, lengthwise. With a sharp knife, slice the rolls straight down into ⅜-inch-thick slices. Pour some sauce onto each of 8 serving plates. Arrange the rounds of salmon across the sauce. Garnish with a few fresh basil leaves.

Steamed New Potatoes

Use very small new potatoes, scrub them well and leave the skin on. Steam them until they are very soft in the middle when tested with a fork. Drain and cut into halves quickly while still in the pan, and serve with plenty of butter and salt and pepper to taste.

Fresh Haricots Verts

If you can't find true *haricots verts*, the best substitute is fresh green beans that have been frenched. Frenching beans is a true pain, particularly because the method originated in a vain attempt to duplicate the delicious French beans that are so thin and crisp just as they grow. If you can't find them this time, vow to grow your own next year, or put pressure on the produce manager of your local market and insist he carry them. Steam or boil them in a small amount of water until they are just *al dente*, and serve with melted butter and salt and pepper to taste on a small side plate with the potatoes.

Tomato and Dill Salad

SERVES 8

To skin the tomatoes, pour boiling water over them (in a pan), let them sit 2 minutes, refresh with cold running water, and the skins will slide right off.

Cut tomatoes in thick slices, sprinkle with very little sugar, let stand 5 minutes, and then sprinkle the chopped dill over them. Meanwhile, put into a bowl the egg yolk, ½ teaspoon salt, cayenne, mustard, chili pepper, lemon rind, and garlic. Mix well and add oil slowly. Then mix in cream, salt to taste, and the beaten egg white. Mix lightly with tomatoes and serve.

5 large skinned tomatoes
Pinch sugar
2 tablespoons chopped fresh dill
1 egg yolk
½ teaspoon salt
Cayenne pepper
1 egg white, beaten until stiff
½ teaspoon dry mustard
Pinch chili pepper
Grated rind of 1 lemon
1 crushed garlic clove
½ cup salad oil
3 tablespoons cream

Cointreau Sponge with Blueberries and Peaches

SERVES 8 TO 10 AMPLY

DOUGH

2 cups all-purpose flour
6 tablespoons warm milk
2 tablespoons sugar
1 envelope dry yeast
Pinch of salt
6 tablespoons (¾ stick) butter,
  at room temperature
4 eggs
2 tablespoons raisins, plumped
  in water and drained

This is one of the most delicious summer desserts you will ever create. It is time consuming but worth it. It can be made as much as a day ahead of time. Its flavor will improve overnight.

Generously butter an 8-cup ring mold and large mixing bowl. Set aside.

Combine ½ cup flour, milk, sugar, yeast, and salt in small mixing bowl and beat until smooth. Let stand until frothy, about 25 minutes.

Combine remaining flour, butter, and eggs in another mixing bowl and blend well. Add yeast mixture and beat until dough is smooth and elastic, 3 to 4 minutes. Add raisins and blend well. Turn into prepared bowl, cover with a tea towel and let rise in a warm place until it has doubled, 45 to 60 minutes.

Punch dough down and transfer to prepared mold, filling evenly. Cover and let rise in a warm place until dough reaches top of mold, about 45 minutes.

About 15 minutes before baking, preheat oven to 375°. Bake until sponge cake is golden and knife inserted in the center comes out clean, about 20 minutes.

While the cake is baking, prepare the syrup. Combine water and sugar in a heavy-bottomed medium saucepan. Bring to a boil over high heat, stirring until sugar dissolves, then boil 3 minutes. Remove from heat and add Cointreau and cognac.

When sponge cake is done, unmold onto a round serving platter and, using a sharp, long-pronged cooking fork, punch holes all over the sides and top of the cake. Spoon (or use a basting tube) the syrup over the warm cake, repeating every 10 to 15 minutes until all the syrup is absorbed. Set aside.

To make the glaze, combine the apricot preserves, water, and zest in a small heavy-bottomed saucepan over medium heat and cook, stirring occasionally, until preserves are melted. Remove from heat and stir in liqueur. Strain sauce through a fine sieve. Spread evenly over the sponge cake. Fill the center with the fruit and serve the crème fraîche in a separate bowl.

You can do all of this in the morning or the day before up to the point of putting the fruit in the center of the sponge ring. Add it just before serving. To serve, cut the cake with a serrated knife, spoon some of the fruit over it, and ladle some crème fraîche on top. You will receive raves and as much applause as the star of the play.

SYRUP

3 cups water
2¼ cups sugar
½ cup Cointreau
3 tablespoons cognac

GLAZE

One 11-ounce jar apricot
  preserves
¼ cup water
Grated zest of 1 lemon
2 tablespoons Cointreau

FILLING

1 cup fresh blueberries and 1 cup fresh peaches, skinned and sliced, or 2 cups blueberries (If you prefer you can use seedless grapes, halved and pitted Bing cherries, halved strawberries, or any combination to make two cups.)

TOPPING

crème fraîche (Mix together ¾ cup heavy whipping cream and ¾ cup commercial sour cream. Let stand, uncovered, at room temperature for at least 4 hours. Chill.)

TWENTY-FOUR

A SAFARI LUNCHEON IN BOTSWANA

August

CAMP MACHABA TERRINE OF DOVE

◆

SOUR FRENCH CORNICHONS

◆

HOWLEY WHITE BREAD WITH BUTTER

◆

STERLING NAPA VALLEY CABERNET SAUVIGNON

◆

SPINACH SALAD À LA SAFARI SOUTH

◆

ORANGE MARMALADE SOUFFLÉ WITH RUM VANILLA SAUCE

Botswana is ideal in August. It's cool at night, sunny and dry in the daytime. It's also a paradise for bird watching, game viewing, fly fishing, and bird shooting. On a typical afternoon dove shoot, eight guns can bag enough to feed everyone in the three (small) villages on the way back to camp, with enough left over to make Dove Terrine for the guests and staff.

The camp waiters, in burgundy coats with black trim and matching burgundy fezzes with black tassels, deftly serve thick slices of this delicious terrine for luncheon. It is accompanied by a really different-tasting spinach salad with peanut butter in the dressing, home-made white bread, and an excellent African red wine.

It all makes one feel so sorry for Ernest Hemingway's characters; they obviously went into the bush with the wrong outfitters. Francis Macomber's wife would have gained ten pounds happily, and Death would have gotten his bicycle stuck in the sand just outside the mess tent. Not only are the Real Men there, but they eat, among other things, broccoli quiche, tigerfish mousse, and dove terrine.

In Africa, the bag would be a mix of Cape turtle, red eye, and laughing dove. Our American mourning dove is closest in size to the laughing dove and you can figure it will take about 14 to 16 birds of this size to make a pound of breast meat.

You can substitute an equal weight of squab, goose, or duck. This recipe will fill 1 large bread-loaf pan or two smaller oval terrines. It will keep 7 to 10 days in the refrigerator and freezes well, but loses a little in texture and flavor compared to a fresh terrine that has been cured 2 days.

Camp Machaba Terrine of Dove

MAKES 1 LARGE BREAD LOAF-SIZE TERRINE
OR 2 SMALLER TERRINES

Preheat oven to 350°.

Cut meat off the bones and remove skin. For the next step, a hand-operated grinder is best, but you can use a food processor. Chop the onion and garlic first and then add the dove and liver, running the processor for only 5 seconds. It should be roughly processed.

In a large bowl, mix the sausage, wine, tarragon, and spices and then add the dove mixture, blending very thoroughly. Line the loaf pan or terrine with bacon, leaving it draped over the edge so you can fold the strips over the top of the meat.

Tightly cover with foil first and then cover with the lid, if there is one. Place the terrines or loaf pan in a shallow baking pan and pour hot water into the pan to a level at least halfway up the sides of the terrines and cook for 1 hour.

After cooking allow the terrine to cool first, then remove any lids, leaving foil in place, and weight down with canned goods or rocks and refrigerate overnight. Remove from the pan the following day and wrap in plastic wrap or foil. Allow to cure for at least 1 more day before serving. The flavors mellow and soften with curing—don't do yourself a disservice by eating it right away.

1 pound dove breasts (14 to 16 mourning doves)
1 medium onion
2 cloves garlic
¼ pound chicken livers
2 eggs
½ pound back fat or fatty bacon
½ pound pork sausage in bulk
¼ cup dry red wine
½ teaspoon dried tarragon (If fresh, use 1 teaspoon, minced.)
¼ teaspoon freshly ground nutmeg
¼ teaspoon freshly ground cloves
1 teaspoon salt
¼ teaspoon freshly ground pepper

Sour French Cornichons

You can buy these in any good food specialty store or, if you have a garden, try growing your own—the pickles are easy to make. For real French seeds, write or call:

Herb Gathering, Inc.
5742 Kenwood
Kansas City, Missouri   64110

Telephone (816) 523-2653.

Have on hand at least 35 small cucumbers 1½ to 2 inches long before you start this recipe. Pick them fresh every day and refrigerate them, unwashed, in a covered jar until you have enough.

35 cornichons, or small cucumbers 1½ to 2 inches long
Salt
1½ cups distilled white vinegar
8 to 10 tiny white pickled onions (Gibson type)
1 green bell pepper
1 red bell pepper
2 sprigs fresh tarragon
2 sprigs fresh thyme
4 large garlic cloves, peeled and halved, with any green center sprouts removed

Rub cornichons with your thumb under running water to remove the tiny spines or warts, and drain in a colander. In a large bowl place one layer of cornichons, sprinkle salt over them and continue layering until all cucumbers are used. Cover and marinate at room temperature for 24 hours.

Rinse well and dry on paper towels. Place in a dry bowl. Combine 1½ cups distilled white vinegar with ⅔ cup water, and bring to a boil. Pour boiling liquid over cucumbers and cover. Marinate another 24 hours. They will look yellowish.

Have 2 pint jars with lids sterilized and ready. Julienne the peppers.

Strain the liquid into an enamel pan and bring to a boil. Add the cornichons and boil 1 minute. Remove pickles with tongs and pack into the jars, each with a sprig of fresh tarragon, some tiny onions, slices of the green and red peppers, two garlic cloves, and a thyme sprig.

Pour the boiling vinegar mixture over the cornichons to within ¼ inch of the top and seal with the hot lids. Let cure for at least 4 weeks and then chill before serving.

Howley White Bread

This is a fine-grained bread with a chewy texture akin to English muffins. The egg yolk and water glaze develop a good crust. It slices well and is delicious toasted. While the classic French baguette is the usual accompaniment for terrines and pâtés, this makes a nice variation. It freezes well and makes the best Bread Pudding (*which see*) by far.
Preheat oven to 375°.

Measure into a large mixing bowl the 2¾ cups warm water. Add, stirring to dissolve, 2 packages dry yeast. Stir in the sugar, salt, and soft butter. Stir in and beat until smooth 3 cups sifted flour. Mix in 3½ cups additional flour.

Form dough into a ball, place in a lightly buttered bowl, and cover with a tea towel or waxed paper. Let rise in a warm place until double in bulk, about 30 minutes. Stir and beat batter down for 30 seconds. Divide dough in half, put into 2 greased bread pans, and let rise for 30 minutes.

Brush the tops of the dough with egg yolk beaten with 1 tablespoon water and a pinch of salt. Bake for 40 minutes. The loaf should sound hollow when tapped if it is done. Remove the loaves from oven, lay them on their sides in the pans for 10 minutes to cool, then slide them out of the pans and cool to room temperature before wrapping in plastic wrap or foil.

2¾ cups warm water
2 packages dry yeast
3 tablespoons sugar
1 tablespoon salt
2 tablespoons soft butter
6½ cups enriched flour, sifted
1 egg yolk
1 tablespoon cool water
Pinch salt

Spinach Salad à la Safari South

SERVES 6 TO 8

1 pound fresh spinach leaves
  (large, if possible)
12 strips of bacon (thick sliced),
  cut into ½-inch lengths
2 cloves of garlic, peeled
  (optional)
10 slices of white bread, cubed
  (optional), or 1 cup of
  prepared garlic croutons
½ cup walnuts or pecans,
  coarsely chopped

Wash and dry the spinach and remove its stems. Stack 5 or 6 leaves on top of each other and roll them up like a cigar. Shred finely with a knife. Store this in a plastic bag in the refrigerator while frying the bacon. Fry bacon until crisp and then drain on paper towels and set aside. Use bacon fat to fry croutons with the 2 cloves of garlic, until the bread is crisp and browned. Stir occasionally to prevent scorching. Discard the 2 garlic pieces and wrap the croutons in paper towels to drain. Just before serving, toss the shredded leaves with ½ cup of nuts and the bacon, and then drizzle dressing lightly. Scatter croutons on top.

Dressing

1 cup of extra virgin olive oil
⅓ cup of raspberry vinegar
1 tablespoon of prepared Dijon
  mustard
1 tablespoon of peanut butter
  (smooth)
2 cloves of garlic, peeled and
  crushed
¼ teaspoon of salt, with freshly
  ground pepper to taste
½ teaspoon sugar

Shake all ingredients well in a quart jar.

Orange Marmalade Soufflé

This soufflé could be made over a campfire. The important thing to remember is to cook it above just-simmering water, not wildly boiling water. It will hold for at least 15 minutes if the meal is delayed. For variation, it can also be made with lime or grapefruit marmalades.

The soufflé should be dome-shaped and much prettier if you use a double boiler that has a top pan with a rounded, not a flat bottom.

Lightly butter the inside lid and the interior of the top pan of a 4-cup double boiler. Spread 2 tablespoons marmalade over the butter. Sprinkle the same surfaces with 2 tablespoons granulated sugar. Set aside, uncovered.

Beat egg whites until stiff, add 3 tablespoons sugar, and beat 1 minute more. Fold a little of the egg whites into the 6 tablespoons marmalade and then fold this lightened mixture into the rest of the egg whites.

Put the lower part of the double boiler on the heat and bring the water to a simmer.

Pour mixture into the prepared top of the double boiler and set over lower pan on heat. Cover, and leave simmering gently for 45 minutes. This is the strongest soufflé you've ever seen. If it pushes the lid of the pan up, don't worry. Just try to ignore it.

Check the bottom pan a few times to make sure there is still enough water in it. Add a little boiling water if it needs it. While the soufflé is cooking, make Rum Vanilla Sauce.

6 tablespoons orange marmalade, plus 2 tablespoons for the pan

6 egg whites

3 tablespoons sugar plus 2 tablespoons for pan and lid

Rum Vanilla Sauce

SERVES 6 TO 8

3 egg yolks
¾ cup confectioner's sugar
3 tablespoons light rum
1 tablespoon vanilla extract
1 cup heavy cream, whipped, or
   1 cup softened vanilla ice
   cream

Beat the yolks. Add sugar, rum, and vanilla, and blend thoroughly. Fold in cream.

When ready to serve, remove the top pan with the soufflé from heat and wipe off any water. Put a warmed plate over the pan, invert, and unmold soufflé. Pour Rum Vanilla Sauce into a sauce boat and serve alongside the soufflé.

TWENTY-FIVE

HOUSE PARTY: SHOOTING IN CUMBRIA

September

AVOCADO SOUP WITH GARLIC MELBA TOAST

◆

ROAST PHEASANT ACCOMPANIED BY BREAD SAUCE
AND BUTTERED BREAD CRUMBS

◆

ORANGE-POTATO SOUFFLÉ

◆

BRUSSELS SPROUTS VINAIGRETTE

◆

FRENCH RED BURGUNDY

◆

LANCASHIRE LEMON SOUFFLÉ

My loader weighed 20 stone (or all of 280 pounds). He was dressed in impeccable tweeds: breeks, waistcoat, jacket, and matching hat. He wore heavy wool knee socks fastened with garters, the swallowtail tabs of which correctly showed just one and one-half inches below the fold of the sock at his knee. His cordovan shoes were polished to mirror brightness. I could see the reflection of my awestruck face in them even though it was raining cats and dogs.

I drew a numbered brass marker from the mahogany case the gamekeeper held out to me. It was number seven, in the Wood.

"A difficult butt, madam," offered Gordon. I think he felt as apprehensive as I. Only the evening before it had been casually mentioned that I would be the first woman, ever, to shoot in the line at Dallam Tower. Knowing the estate had belonged to our host's family since the eleventh century, I felt a certain amount of pressure—approximately nine centuries' worth.

I was determined to get the first bird that came down the hill through the trees. I just prayed it was a pheasant because I knew what a pheasant looked like, even though I had never been on a driven pheasant shoot before in my life. I was worried about shooting one of the prized white pheasants, which was a no-no. Suffice it to say, I did get the first bird. It was a pheasant, and it landed stone dead right at my loader's feet.

The final evening during dinner a gallant brigadier rose and told a story on himself. It seemed his wife had been loading for him on a drive that lasted one hour and five minutes (the beating was superb). We had been requested by our host to use only one gun on this drive and they had gotten very hot. The brigadier turned to his wife and requested his second gun to replace his overheated one.

"Certainly not, Charles!" she responded. "Mrs. Perkins in the next blind is outshooting you and *she* doesn't have a second gun with *her*. Shame! It wouldn't be sportsmanlike." So saying, he raised his glass and drank a toast to the first lady ever to shoot on the line at Dallam Tower. Of such chivalrous gestures are fond friends and memories made.

Avocado Soup

SERVES 6

Peel and seed the avocados. Put them in a blender or food processor with the lemon juice, onion, and chicken stock, and purée. Remove the mixture from the processor and pour into a large bowl. Whisk in the sour cream and then the light cream. Add the salt and pepper, taste and adjust the seasonings if necessary. Put into a double boiler and heat. Or serve chilled with a sprinkle of chopped parsley on top.

Garlic toast is perfect with this creamy, lightly flavored soup.

3 cups chicken stock (canned broth is all right.)
3 cups light cream
4 large ripe avocados
3 tablespoons lemon juice
⅔ cup sour cream
½ teaspoon salt
¼ teaspoon white pepper
2 tablespoons minced onion

Garlic Melba Toast

SERVES 4 TO 6

Preheat over to 350°.

Blend 4 tablespoons soft butter with 1 clove of garlic, which has been put through a garlic press. Spread on 6 slices of very thin white bread with crusts removed. Cut in halves or quarters to form triangles, and bake in a 350° oven for 7 to 8 minutes. If the toast isn't totally crisp, turn off the oven and let it sit another 15 minutes. Cool and store in a covered tin if not serving right away.

House Party: Shooting in Cumbria

Roast Pheasant

Preheat oven to 350°.

One bird for 2 people will be ample. If fresh, the pheasant should have been hung 4 or 5 days under refrigeration before cooking. If it has been frozen, thaw it completely to room temperature.

Clip off the wings at the first joint, legs at the joint, and the neck close to the body. Liver and heart may be used for pâté or for another recipe.

Place the birds in an open pan with a splash of water, breast side up. Cover the breast with 4 full strips of bacon. Place in a preheated oven at 350° for 35 to 45 minutes, depending on size. Test for doneness with the Thermicator. The internal temperature should be 140° to 150°. We recommend 140° for the best flavor and moistness. Remove from heat and let rest for 10 or 15 minutes before carving. The bird will continue to cook while it is standing, so if you want a pale pink center remove it from the oven at 140°.

Bread Sauce

½ small loaf white bread, crust removed
3 cloves
1 cup milk
1 teaspoon salt and freshly ground pepper to taste
2 tablespoons butter
3 small onions

Put the bread, broken in pieces, into a heavy-bottomed saucepan with the salt, pepper, butter, and milk. Cut the onion into halves and stick the 3 cloves into 3 of the halves and put all the onion pieces into the saucepan. Bring the mixture to a boil and stir. Lower the heat and simmer for 2 minutes, stirring gently. Set aside for 1 hour, then reheat. Remove the onion and cloves, stir well, and serve in a sauce boat. This is the traditional English accompaniment for all kinds of game and poultry. It is always served with:

Buttered Bread Crumbs

Crush the dried bread with a rolling pin, then rub through a wire sieve. Melt the butter in a small frying pan and stir crumbs in the butter over medium heat until browned and crisp. Serve in a small bowl next to the Bread Sauce and pheasant.

Orange-Potato Soufflé

SERVES 6

Preheat oven to 375°.

Peel the potatoes and cube roughly. Boil in 1 cup of water for 15 minutes, or until they feel soft when pierced with a fork. Drain the water off and place the potatoes in a food processor, or you may mash them by hand. Add the orange rind, butter, hot milk, and salt and pepper. Beat with an electric mixer or run food processor for 8 to 10 seconds, until the potatoes are creamy.

Beat the egg whites until stiff, and fold a small amount of them into the potato mixture to lighten it, and then pour the entire potato mixture into the egg whites and fold in carefully. Pour into a buttered 4-cup soufflé dish and bake for 25 minutes until it is puffed and golden brown on top. Serve immediately.

This dish is also very good with duck instead of the traditional wild rice, for a change. The hint of orange flavor underscores the natural affinity between wild duck and orange.

6 Idaho potatoes
Grated rind of 1 navel orange
6 egg whites
6 tablespoons butter
¼ cup hot milk
1 teaspoon salt
Freshly ground pepper to taste

Brussels Sprouts Vinaigrette

SERVES 6

Steam the brussels sprouts until cooked but still firm, about 6 or 7 minutes. Keep them warm in the steamer with the heat turned off.

Heat 1 tablespoon of the olive oil in a small skillet and sauté the garlic over medium-low heat for 3 minutes, stirring constantly. Do not let it brown. Add the remaining ingredients and cook for 1 minute longer, stirring all the time.

Put the steamed, drained brussels sprouts in a heated dish and pour the sauce over them, stirring lightly to

1 pound of the smallest brussels sprouts you can find
¼ cup oil
2 garlic cloves, peeled and put through a garlic press
1 tablespoon sherry vinegar
1 teaspoon lemon juice
3 scallions, finely chopped
1 large green bell pepper, finely chopped

mix. Serve at once.

Brussels sprouts are not a popular vegetable, and in my opinion it's because they are overgrown in this country. They should be about the size of your little fingernail, no larger. The taste and texture are superb when they are this size. They're hardly the thing one can grow in a windowbox, but if you have a garden, plant some. Harvest them from the bottom of the stalk first when they are tiny. The upper ones will be barely discernible at this time; leave them to grow until they reach the tiny size. Down with the overblown little cabbages that we see so often in the market!

Lancashire Lemon Soufflé

SERVES 6

3 lemons
3 large eggs
½ packet unflavored gelatin
(1½ teaspoons)
¾ cup confectioner's sugar

Separate the eggs and beat the yolks until frothy. Grate the rind of two lemons and beat into the yolks with the sugar. Beat with an electric beater or by hand until creamy and smooth.

Squeeze the juice of all the lemons and beat in gradually. Dissolve the gelatin in ½ cup warm water and add to the mixture, then strain into a clean bowl.

Beat the egg whites until stiff and carefully fold them into the yolk mixture. Pour into a 2-cup soufflé dish and chill in the refrigerator at least 2 hours.

This is a relatively low-calorie dessert and it has a very tart, lively flavor, which is most welcome after a full dinner such as this. The recipe was given to me by the cook at Underley Grange in Lancashire when I sought her out in the kitchen after dinner one evening, exclaiming upon its lightness and refreshing flavor.

TWENTY-SIX

PERDIX PERDIX PERDIX IN DENMARK

September

BRIE BAKED IN CRUST

◆

AQUAVIT AND DANISH BEER

◆

ROAST HUNGARIAN PARTRIDGE

◆

CABBAGE STRUDEL

◆

GREEN PEPPER AND WALNUT SALAD WITH FETA CHEESE
AND OLIVES

◆

BREAD PUDDING WITH LEMON SAUCE

The last day's shooting on a trip to Denmark involved crossing the Bay of Svendborg by motor launch to the four-thousand-acre Skaro Island, where we were invited to shoot the opening day of the partridge season. The European grey partridge is a very sporty flier, and these were to be all wild birds.

My beat was right on the beach and the birds would streak out over a high dune on my left toward the open water on my right. The trick was to drop them immediately, on the beach. If their momentum carried them too far out over the water they would be lost, swept away by the strong currents before a dog could get to them. I'm not too fond of going-away shots, so I was very happy.

The food was outstanding on this trip. A typical luncheon offered three kinds of herring with dark bread, smoked salmon, smoked eel, a poached fish with sauce, roast chicken, smoked ham, roast pork with caramelized apples, various salads and vegetables, and, of course, Danish pastries. All accompanied by aquavit and beer throughout the entire meal.

Each day's shooting would be on a different estate. At Edderup Skovgaard, the first course included an outstanding cheese, baked in a thin crust and garnished with walnuts. It could have been the entire luncheon with a green salad. Of course it was only one part of the first course.

The partridge are commonly known as Hungarian partridge or, even more common, Huns, so I've chosen to use another Hungarian dish with them, Cabbage Strudel. You could have a tossed salad with this instead of the pepper and walnuts, but don't skip the dessert. It's easy, light, and homely, in the most comforting sense of the word.

Brie Baked in Crust

SERVES 6 TO 8 AS A CANAPÉ

Preheat oven to 400°.

Put the flour and salt in a food processor with a steel blade. Scatter the butter pats around on the flour. Use the on-off technique until the butter is cut into the dough thoroughly. Turn on the machine and pour the ice water through the feed tube all at once. Run the machine until the dough masses into a ball. Remove dough and wrap it in plastic wrap or foil and put it in the refrigerator for 15 minutes to rest.

Put the cheese in the freezer.

Roll out dough on a lightly floured board to ¼-inch thickness. Remove the cheese from freezer and wrap it in the dough, pinching the edges to seal. Cut off the excess. The dough is very pliable, but if it tears put a patch of dough over the tear and push your fingers across it to repair. The cheese should be completely covered.

If the wrapping process takes you more than 2 or 3 minutes, replace the wrapped cheese in the freezer for 5 or 6 minutes to chill again.

Remove from freezer and brush top and sides of dough with the yolk-water mixture. Put the walnut halves on top and place in the preheated oven. Bake for 15 minutes. Remove from the oven and allow to cool for 2 or 3 minutes before cutting.

The cheese could be cut into smaller portions and wrapped in the dough individually if you would like to serve them on separate plates as a cheese course.

1 pound Brie cheese in a wedge or small round
1 cup white all-purpose flour
1 stick (¼ pound) butter, cut into 12 pats
¼ cup ice water
½ teaspoon salt
Yolk of 1 egg, beaten with 1 teaspoon cold water and a pinch of salt
8 to 10 walnut halves

Roast Hungarian Partridge

ALLOW 1 BIRD PER SERVING

Preheat oven to 350°.

Place the properly hung (see Appendix) oven-ready birds in an open pan, breast side up, with a splash of water. Place 3 half strips of bacon over the breast and put in a preheated oven for approximately 25 to 30 minutes. The internal temperature is critical and should be 140° to 150° when done. The latter temperature is well done; do not cook the bird any longer or it will become tough, dry, and flavorless. Allow it to rest outside the oven for 5 to 10 minutes before carving.

Cabbage Strudel

SERVES 6 TO 8

Start the evening before you want to serve this dish by removing your filo dough from the freezer and placing it in the refrigerator to defrost. If you don't have overnight, the dough should be defrosted outside the refrigerator for at least 4 hours.

Another thing to start the evening before is the cabbage. You will need a large head. Shred it finely, place it in a bowl, sprinkle the salt over it, and let it stand, covered, overnight.

I am assuming that you are familiar with frozen filo dough. Buy it. It's hysterical fun to make your own, but hardly any of us needs *that* much fun. Have a damp tea towel ready to place over the unused leaves of dough as you remove each one. It dries very fast and becomes unusable in no time. Have a buttered, shallow, ovenproof baking dish (9 × 12 inches) ready.

6 sheets of filo dough
4 tablespoons sweet butter, melted
2½ pounds cabbage (1 large head)
1 tablespoon salt
4 tablespoons olive oil
1 tablespoon sugar
½ teaspoon freshly ground pepper

Preheat oven to 375°.

With your hands or in a tea towel, squeeze the cabbage (which has stood overnight) well to eliminate most of the liquid extracted by the salt.

Heat the oil in a large frying pan, add the sugar, and brown it slightly while stirring.

Add the drained cabbage. Stir it immediately for about 1 minute, lower the heat, and cook it without a cover until it is golden brown. Melt the 4 tablespoons butter and have a pastry brush at hand.

Now unwrap the filo dough and lay if flat on a counter, with the dampened tea towel ready. Remove 1 sheet, place it in the dish so that it just covers the bottom, letting the rest of it hang over the edge. Brush it with the melted butter. Place the next sheet with the excess dough hanging over the other side of the dish. Brush with the melted butter. Repeat, staggering each layer, until you have 6 layers in the bottom of the dish.

160

Place the cooked cabbage on top of the strudel dough. Grind the pepper over it, and cover with the flaps of filo left hanging over the edges of the dish. As you fold each one over the filling, brush it with melted butter. Place in the preheated oven for 30 minutes, or until a delicately browned on top. Cut into squares for serving.

Green Pepper and Walnut Salad with Feta Cheese and Olives

SERVES 6

Preheat oven to 300°.

If you have a gas stove, put the whole peppers 1 at a time on the tines of a long-handled fork and turn them over a flame until the skin blisters and darkens. If you have an electric oven, place the peppers on a baking sheet and broil them about 3 inches from the heat, turning them so all sides are colored.

Remove from heat and wrap the peppers in a damp towel for 5 minutes. Rub them with the towel and the burned skins will slip off.

Cut the peppers in half, remove seeds, white membrane, and stems. Julienne them in ½-inch-wide strips. Oil a shallow baking dish large enough to hold the pepper strips in one layer. Sprinkle the onions evenly over them and bake in the oven for 30 minutes. Remove from the oven, place on paper towels, and cool.

Meanwhile, put the walnuts into a food processor, mortar, or nutgrinder and pulverize them. Add the garlic, salt, freshly ground pepper, and vinegar. Mix thoroughly and then add the oil slowly. Taste for seasoning and adjust, if necessary, with more salt or pepper.

Pour the walnut dressing over the peppers and chill or leave at room temperature, as you wish.

When ready to serve, line a salad bowl or individual serving plates with the lettuce. Arrange the pepper strips and scallions over it, and sprinkle the crumbled feta cheese and the olives over the top. Serve this as a separate course, following the partridge and cabbage strudel.

6 medium-sized bell peppers, green and red
1 head Boston lettuce
⅔ cup olive oil
4 tablespoons red wine vinegar
1 teaspoon salt
1 garlic clove, put through a garlic press
Freshly ground black pepper
½ cup walnuts
6 green scallions, finely chopped
12 Kalamata olives, or ripe black olives
1 cup feta cheese, crumbled

Bread Pudding with Lemon Sauce

SERVES 6 TO 8

4 *slices Howley White Bread*
  (which see), buttered
2 cups milk
4 eggs
Dash salt
⅓ cup sugar
1 teaspoon vanilla

SAUCE

Rind of 2 lemons, grated
½ cup lemon juice
½ cup water
1 tablespoon cornstarch
3 tablespoons sugar

Preheat oven to 300°.

Cut off the crusts, butter the bread, cube it, and place it in a buttered bread-loaf pan. Beat together the eggs, salt and sugar. Add the milk and vanilla and mix thoroughly.

Pour the milk mixture over the bread cubes in the pan and place the loaf pan in a bain-marie. Place the bain-marie on medium heat on top of the stove and heat the water just to the boiling point. Do not boil.

Place the bain-marie with its contents into the preheated oven and bake for 50 to 55 minutes.

Grate the lemon rind into a heavy saucepan. Add the juice and sugar. Mix the cornstarch with the water, add to the juice mixture, and stir well. Bring to the boiling point, stirring constantly until clarified and thickened slightly. Cool to room temperature.

Remove the pudding from the oven when a knife inserted into it comes out clean. Remove from the water bath and cool to room temperature.

At serving time, spoon the pudding into individual serving dishes, ladle the lemon sauce over it. This is the kind of food that nourishes your soul as well as your body.

162

TWENTY-SEVEN

DOVE SHOOTING IN GEORGIA

September

ROAST DOVE

◆

BAKED BARLEY CASSEROLE

◆

SPINACH PIE

◆

BANANA MOUSSE

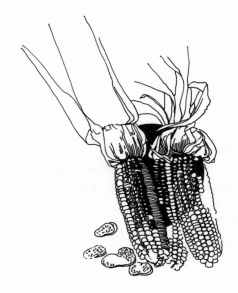

A dove shoot can be a large social event as well as a good test of one's ability with a shotgun. (Dropping one out of four birds is considered good shooting.) If the dove field is large enough and the weather has favored the farmer with good crops of feed, it's possible to invite thirty-five to forty guests to luncheon and have the dove shoot following. The benne (sesame) field could cover 25 to 30 acres, with the blinds placed in rows around it, through it, and under trees.

There is usually corn planted around the outside of the benne, and in the middle an acre or so of peanuts, in which a hog is allowed to root around and dig up the peanuts on the previous day. He drops a lot of them as he munches away, so there are many broken ones left on the ground for the doves.

One always wears one's best shooting outfit for the occasion, and takes a pick-up boy as well as his best-behaved retriever.

At one plantation, upon arriving at the designated blind, and while the rest of the guns are taking their places, one can watch a man on horseback who starts in the middle of the field. He rides in ever-increasing concentric circles. As he goes around he calls, "*coo-eee, coo-eee,*" to keep the doves out of the field until everyone is placed. Finally, his circles widen out until he disappears into the tall pines surrounding the field, and the shoot commences.

Roast Dove

ALLOW 2 BIRDS PER SERVING

Preheat oven to 475°.

Many epicures consider the dove the finest of all game birds. Fortunately, it is difficult to spoil them by overcooking, but again, internal temperature is the best guideline to doneness.

For hanging and plucking instructions, see Appendix.

Birds should be at room temperature. Place the cleaned dove in a roasting pan, on its side. Put a splash of water in the pan, but not enough to cover the bottom of the pan. Cover the breasts with a short strip of bacon. After 4 minutes, turn the dove to the other side, shifting the bacon to the top, and continue roasting for an additional 4 minutes.

Test the dove with the Thermicator. At 140° internal temperature the center will be light pink (our preference), and at 150° the center will be brown all the way through but still moist and good.

Because the cooking time for dove is short, prepare everything else on the menu first. Please notice that the Barley Casserole must be started the evening before by soaking the navy beans.

Baked Barley Casserole

SERVES 4 TO 6

Preheat oven to 350.

The flavor of this dish is dependent upon the quality of your stock. Do make your own if possible. It does make a difference. Just buy 3 pounds of chicken backs and necks and simmer them in 2½ quarts of water for 1½ hours with all of the celery leaves cut from a bunch of celery, or 2 roughly chopped celery stalks. Toss in one bay leaf, 4 sprigs of fresh parsley, ½ teaspoon dried thyme, or 2 sprigs fresh thyme. Don't cover it and don't add salt. The liquid should reduce to 1½ quarts.

Discard chicken and herbs and strain the stock through a fine sieve. Measure out 6 cups of stock.

Soak ½ cup navy beans overnight in cold water. Drain the beans and cook them in 1 quart (reserve the rest) of chicken stock or canned broth for 45 minutes, or until they can be pierced easily with a fork. Add 1 cup barley and 2 teaspoons salt and cook over low heat until the barley is tender, about 30 minutes, adding more chicken stock if necessary to keep it from drying out and sticking to the pan. Add the freshly ground white pepper and the 2 tablespoons of butter.

Turn the mixture into a buttered casserole and bake in preheated oven for 25 to 30 minutes. Do not let it brown. It tastes better if it is still a trifle soupy at serving time rather than completely dry. If needed, add a little more stock during the last 5 minutes.

Barley tastes just right with dove. Its nutty flavor complements the bird perfectly, and it's a good change from potatoes or rice. This would also be fitting with pheasant, Cornish game hens, or chicken.

½ cup dried navy beans
1½ quarts chicken stock (or canned broth)
1 cup pearled barley
2 teaspoons salt
Freshly ground white pepper to taste
2 tablespoons butter

Spinach Pie

2 cups fresh spinach, cooked,
  drained, and chopped; or 2
  packages frozen chopped
  spinach, cooked and drained
½ teaspoon salt
Dash white pepper
1 tablespoon chopped, sautéed
  onion
¼ teaspoon freshly grated
  nutmeg
3 tablespoons butter
3 tablespoons flour (potato flour
  if possible)
1½ cups scalded milk
½ cup sharp cheddar cheese,
  grated
One 8-inch pie shell, baked (see
  Onion Tart)

Preheat oven to 350°.

Melt the butter in a heavy saucepan. Add the potato flour and let it bubble for at least 3 minutes to cook the flour. Pour in the scalded milk and whisk vigorously until sauce is thickened. Let simmer another 3 minutes. Remove from heat.

Squeeze all the water out of the cooked spinach in a sieve, pressing with a wooden spoon, and add the spinach to the cream sauce. Add the salt and pepper, sautéed onion, and freshly ground nutmeg. Mix well and pour the spinach mixture into the baked pie shell.

Sprinkle the top with the grated cheese. Place in the preheated oven for 25 to 30 minutes. Cool for 10 to 15 minutes before cutting into wedges. It is good warm or at room temperature.

Banana Mousse

3 medium-ripe bananas
½ cup fresh strawberries
4 tablespoons sugar or
  equivalent sugar substitute
½ teaspoon vanilla extract
3 egg whites stiffly beaten
1½ teaspoons unflavored gelatin
Juice of 1 lemon

Dissolve the gelatin in the lemon juice by mixing together in a small cup set in a pan of hot water. Purée 2 of the 3 bananas with the gelatin and lemon mixture in a food processor, or mash very thoroughly with a fork. Add 3 tablespoons of sweetener (reserving one for garnish), and the vanilla. Stiffly beat the egg whites and fold into the banana mixture. Place ½ of the banana-egg-white mixture into a 4-cup soufflé dish. Put a layer of sliced bananas over this and then add the other half of the mousse mixture.

Refrigerate for at least 1 hour. Evenly sprinkle the remaining tablespoon of sweetener over the top of the mousse, then place halved strawberries on top for garnish. This low-calorie dessert tastes great, even if you are not on a diet.

TWENTY-EIGHT

DON'T COOK THIS IN A DOUBLE BOILER

October

PHEASANT POACHED IN CREAM

◆

GREEN TOMATO PIE

◆

ACORN SQUASH STUFFED WITH WILD RICE

◆

BURGESS NAPA VALLEY CHARDONNAY

◆

BELGIAN ENDIVE SALAD

◆

APPLE MERINGUE WITH RED CURRANT SAUCE

This is one of the easiest and most delicious ways to prepare pheasant or ruffed grouse. Even chicken works, but it needs extra seasoning of basil and nutmeg, to taste. The meat is moist and tender and the cream absorbs the flavor of the bird, really enhancing it.

I put this recipe in the March 1984 *Orvis News* and, like a fool, I didn't recook it to refresh my memory before I wrote out the recipe. We had prepared it count-less times, and it's so simple I just dashed it off and left for Tasmania.

Upon my return, I had some nonfan mail waiting for me. One message in particular stands out in my mind. It seems that a Gentleman with a Pheasant read the recipe and decided to use it. He put the pheasant pieces in the double boiler (as I instructed), cooked it for fifteen or twenty minutes (as I instructed), and wound up with a cream-covered raw pheasant.

He wrote a note, asking for clarification. It was put in my box and, as I was not there, I did not answer it. A week or so went by and he called the Orvis Company to inquire of one of the telephone operators what he was supposed to do with his half-cooked bird. The plucky lass replied that she surely did not know about that particular recipe, but she knew for a fact that the boss liked his game half raw.

Being admirably persistent, the caller asked to speak to the boss. My long-suffering husband, who had taught me the recipe in the first place, straightened it all out. This dish should be cooked in a heavy tin-lined copper pot directly over the heat. I apologize to my reader and herewith offer the recipe for the second time.

Poached Pheasant in Cream

SERVES 6

Split the breast and disjoint the legs of the bird. Put the 12 pieces of pheasant into a large heavy-bottomed saucepan or frying pan. Cover with the half-and-half and place on low heat. Test the liquid with the Thermicator; it should be 200° when you start timing it. Simmer, uncovered, for 15 to 20 minutes. Turn pieces of pheasant after 10 minutes. The internal temperature should be 140° to 150° when done.

Remove the pheasant pieces, keep them warm, and reduce the cream by boiling to 1½ cups. Stir frequently during this process.

Whisk in the sour cream and cook just long enough to heat through. Place the pheasant pieces on buttered toast and cover with the sauce. Sprinkle a little chopped parsley on top to garnish.

If you have a large amount of sauce left, it makes a delicious base for a soup. Add two finely diced sautéed leeks and 1 large potato, boiled and pushed through a sieve; reheat or chill and eat as vichyssoise, with chopped chives on top.

2 pheasants, cleaned and dressed (see Appendix for cleaning and hanging instructions)
1 quart half-and-half
1 pint sour cream
Salt and pepper
Buttered toast
2 tablespoons chopped parsley for garnish

Green Tomato Pie

SERVES 6

Preheat oven to 400°.

Slice the larger tomatoes in ½-inch slices. If using the cherry or pear tomatoes, halve them. Arrange in the unbaked shell. Mix the sour cream, mayonnaise, and the grated cheese together and pour over the tomatoes. Bake in the preheated oven for 20 minutes. This pie goes well with red meat, fish, or fowl, or it can be served as a luncheon main course with a salad and some crusty bread.

1 unbaked pie shell (see recipe for Onion Tart shell)
7 or 8 medium-sized green tomatoes, or 2 pounds green cherry tomatoes or green pear tomatoes
¼ cup sour cream
¼ cup mayonnaise
¼ cup sharp grated cheese (sharp cheddar or Parmesan)

Acorn Squash Stuffed with Wild Rice

3 acorn squash, halved and
  seeded
2 cups cooked wild rice
½ teaspoon seasoned salt
2 teaspoons grated orange rind
2 large shallots, finely minced
4 tablespoons butter
4 tablespoons orange juice
Freshly ground black pepper

Preheat oven to 350°.

In a large bowl, thoroughly mix together the wild rice, orange rind, salt, and minced shallots. Fill cavities of squash with the mixture. Pour 1 tablespoon orange juice over rice in each squash half and dot with half the butter, reserving the rest. Cover with foil and bake in the preheated oven for 45 to 60 minutes, depending upon the size of the squash. It should be tender when pierced with a fork.

Remove from the oven, dot with the remaining butter, and grind some fresh black pepper on top before serving.

Belgian Endive Salad

⅓ cup peeled, blanched,
  slivered almonds
4 Belgian endives, thinly sliced
  crosswise
2 tablespoons chopped parsley
  for garnish

DRESSING

2 tablespoons almond oil
1 tablespoon fresh lemon juice
1 teaspoon garlic, put through a
  garlic press (1 to 2 cloves)
Salt and pepper to taste

Mix lemon juice and garlic in a bowl. While whisking, pour in oil slowly. Add salt and freshly ground pepper to taste. Pour over salad and toss lightly. Sprinkle chopped parsley on top to garnish.

Apple Meringue with Red Currant Sauce

SERVES 6 AMPLY

This dessert improves in flavor if it is made 1 day ahead of serving.

Preheat oven to 375°.

Peel and core the apples. Slice them ¼ inch thick, put into a bowl and pour the lemon juice over them. Mix well so the lemon juice will prevent the apples from turning brown.

Soak the raisins in the rum to soften them, about 10 to 15 minutes, then strain the rum into the bread crumbs and mix well.

Beat the egg yolks with ½ cup of the sugar until they are a pale yellow color. Beat in the vanilla, cinnamon, and freshly grated nutmeg. Add the rum-bread-crumb mixture, the raisins, the grated orange rind, and the apples. Set aside.

Beat the egg whites with a pinch of salt until they form soft peaks. Gradually add the remaining ¼ cup sugar and beat until the meringue is shiny and firm. Fold ⅓ of the egg whites into the apple mixture to lighten it, and then reverse the process and fold the apple mixture into the egg whites.

Pour the clarified butter into a heavy-bottomed, oven-proof, 1½-quart saucepan with a lid, and set over medium heat. When the butter has heated, pour in the apple mixture. The pan should be about ¾ full. Turn the heat to high for 2 or 3 minutes without stirring the apples. Remove from the heat, cover, and put into the preheated oven for 35 to 40 minutes until the meringue has puffed up and shrunk from the sides of the pan.

Remove from the oven, uncover, and let cool 2 to 3 minutes. Place a serving plate over the pan, invert, and unmold. Allow to cool.

Melt the currant jelly in a small saucepan over low heat. Spoon it over the cooled meringue. Sprinkle the diced cherries on top.

This is a rich-tasting dessert, despite the simplicity of the ingredients. Small servings are ample.

2 pounds Granny Smith apples

1 cup very stale bread crumbs (Make your own with dried French bread, pulverized in a food processor or blender.)

¾ cup dark rum

½ cup golden raisins

3 tablespoons lemon juice

4 eggs, separated

3 cups granulated sugar

Rind of 1 orange, grated

½ teaspoon vanilla extract

1½ teaspoons cinnamon

¼ teaspoon freshly grated nutmeg

Pinch salt

6 tablespoons unsalted butter, clarified (Melt in a small heavy frying pan and pour through a sieve without scraping the pan. The object is to remove the white curds that will burn.)

One 8-ounce jar red currant jelly

4 or 5 candied cherries, finely diced

TWENTY NINE

A SAVOURY AUTUMN DINNER IN VERMONT

October

GRILLED WOODCOCK

◆

SCALLION PANCAKES

◆

TINY BRUSSELS SPROUTS AND MUSHROOMS IN VERMOUTH
SAUCE

◆

STAG'S LEAP VINEYARDS CABERNET SAUVIGNON

◆

PLUM CRUMB

Grilled Woodcock

Woodcock have a distinctive flavor, and if you are doubtful about your guests' fondness for wild meat, serve quail or dove instead.

The European tradition with woodcock is to cook them without removing the innards. There is good reason for this because the woodcock has a large heart and liver. Also, like no other bird except the snipe, the intestines (trail) are good to eat. In both woodcock and snipe the intestines come in a tight little white coil and are always clean.

Leigh used this savoury treat as a test of my ardor, or perhaps, my true grit, before we were married. He simply sautéed the little white coil with the heart and liver and presented it to me on toast. I had to drink two martinis before I got up enough nerve to eat it.

We never cook the woodcock with the innards in, because then it is necessary to overcook the outer bird in order to cook the inner bird properly. The best way to prepare woodcock is to sauté the trail, heart, and liver in 2 or 3 tablespoons of butter over low heat for about 5 minutes, stirring occasionally. Purée or mash them, and add 1 teaspoon of heavy cream, 1 teaspoon of very dry sherry, and salt and pepper for each 3-piece set of giblets. Spread the resulting pâté on toast and serve under the cooked birds. It's really delicious, and much less likely to create anguish in your guests.

Of special interest are woodcock legs. They are white meat and the breast is dark meat. To our knowledge, there is no other bird with this distinction. By all means, pay attention to the legs, the best part of the bird, and the best-eating legs of any bird. See our recipe for Woodcock Legs Sautéed in Garlic Butter.

See the Appendix for cleaning and hanging instructions.

Split the bird down the middle of the breast, not the back, with game shears, and flatten precisely in the same manner as you would break the back of a book. Broil about 5 minutes on each side and test with the Thermicator. The internal temperature should be

130° to 150°, depending on whether you like it rare or more done. Be warned, however, that this bird will get tough if it is overcooked.

Scallion Pancakes

SERVES 6 TO 8

Mix the flour and water together to make a soft dough. With heavily floured hands, divide into 6 pieces and shape roughly into rounds 6 inches across.

Wash and finely chop the scallions. Spread 1 teaspoon oil over each round of dough and sprinkle ⅙ of the scallions on each round. Sprinkle each lightly with salt and roll up tightly like a cigar. Fold each rolled piece of dough in half and twist into a spiral. Flatten with a rolling pin and on a floured board reroll to a round about 6 inches across. This mixes the scallions throughout the dough. Stack on a plate with waxed paper in between each pancake.

Cover the bottom of a large frying pan with oil, heat over a medium flame, and place 1 cake at a time in the pan and fry on each side for 2 minutes to brown it, and then cook for another 3 minutes on each side on very low heat to cook through. Turn the cakes with two spatulas so as not to splatter grease all over yourself.

Put paper towels in the bottom of a large baking pan and place each cake into it as it is cooked. Keep them warm in a low oven. When all are done, cut each pancake into 6 wedges and serve piping hot.

If you want to serve these without using the following vegetable dish with vermouth sauce, accompany the pancakes with tamari soy sauce in small individual bowls into which the pancakes can be dipped before eating.

3 cups flour
1¼ cups water
10 green scallions
6 tablespoons vegetable oil
Salt

Tiny Brussels Sprouts and Mushrooms in Vermouth Sauce

SERVES 6 TO 8

2 cups fresh mushrooms, halved
    if small or medium size,
    quartered if large
2 cups fresh brussels sprouts, as
    small as you can find them
5 tablespoons butter
3 tablespoons oil
1½ cups heavy cream
½ cup dry vermouth, warmed
Salt to taste
Freshly ground white pepper
¾ cup chicken stock (Canned
    broth is all right.)

Remove stems from mushrooms and save for another sauce or soup. Wash the mushrooms quickly in a large bowl of cold water with a splash of vinegar in it, and drain. Pat dry with paper towels. Quarter the mushrooms if they are large, or halve them if smaller.

Heat the oil and butter together in a large frying pan. Add the mushrooms and sauté them over low heat for 8 to 10 minutes. Do not brown. Add more butter while they are cooking, if necessary.

Remove the mushrooms from the pan and keep them warm. Put the vermouth into a small pan and heat for 1 minute over medium-low heat. Light a kitchen match to it, flambé, and pour immediately, while still flaming, into the frying pan. Stir to deglaze the pan of any mushroom pieces and let the flames die down.

Add the cream and reduce to low heat for 8 to 10 minutes until thickened. Add salt and pepper to taste.

Meanwhile, put the brussels sprouts into a saucepan, add the chicken stock or broth, and bring to a boil. Lower the heat and simmer for 5 to 8 minutes, depending on the sprouts' size. They should be bright green and crunchy.

Drain the brussels sprouts well, pat with paper towels to dry further, then add them to the sauce. Add the mushrooms, mix well, and adjust the seasonings if necessary. Serve beside the scallion pancakes on the individual plates, and spoon a little of the vermouth sauce on each pancake, if desired.

If you want to serve this vegetable without the scallion pancakes, put slices of toast beneath each individual serving.

Plum Crumb

SERVES 6 TO 8

Preheat oven to 400°.

Wash plums and place in a large pan. Pour boiling water over them and let stand 2 minutes. Drain in a colander and refresh under cold running water. They should peel easily. Cut the plums off their pits and put the pieces into an enameled or other acid-resistant saucepan. Add the sugar and lemon juice and let stand for 1 hour.

Grind the blanched almonds in a food processor or blender, add the sugar and flour, and while the machine is running, drop in the butter 1 pat at a time. Add the vanilla, run the machine a second or so to mix it in, then remove the mixture to a bowl and set aside.

Put the plums in their pan on medium heat, bring to a boil, then reduce the heat to low and simmer for 20 minutes, uncovered.

Butter a 9-inch square tempered glass or other heat-proof baking dish. Strain the plums, letting their syrup flow into a heavy saucepan. Place the plums in the buttered baking dish and return the syrup to low heat to simmer and reduce for 15 to 20 minutes, until the sauce is thick.

Pour the reduced sauce over the plums and sprinkle half of the crumb mixture over them. Place the baking dish in the preheated oven for 10 minutes.

Remove from the oven, sprinkle the remaining half of the crumb mixture on top of the plums and return to the oven for another 10 minutes, until the top is golden brown. The first baking thickens this dish, the second baking then crisps the final layer of crumbs. Remove from the oven and let cool at least 15 minutes before serving.

This dessert can be made in the morning and served at room temperature for dinner. The top will still be crunchy, as it should be. A day later it is still good, but no longer crisp on top.

If you're in a hurry, or fresh plums are not available, use two 12-ounce jars of Victoria Plum Preserves in-

2 pounds prune plums (Do not use black plums, they are almost impossible to peel.)
½ cup sugar
Juice of 1 lemon, strained
Butter for casserole or baking dish
½ cup almonds, blanched and ground
⅓ cup sugar
½ cup flour
Pinch of salt
4 tablespoons butter (½ stick), cut into 4 pats
1 teaspoon vanilla extract

stead of the fresh plums. Grate the rind of 1 lemon over them, add the juice of ½ lemon, mix well, and place in the baking dish before sprinkling the crumb mixture on top as above. This is a very good substitute, but it's not as good as the real thing, with its tart-sweet freshness.

THIRTY

A DINNER FOR YOUR DEAREST FRIENDS

October

HIGHBUSH CRANBERRY SAUCE

◆

MUSHROOM PIE

◆

ROAST RUFFED GROUSE

◆

WILD RICE

◆

GRGICH HILLS CHARDONNAY

◆

CRÈME BRÛLÉE

In October, the wild highbush cranberries are ripe along roadsides in Vermont. The scarlet fruit hangs in clusters that are sometimes fifteen or twenty feet high. One leaves those for the ruffed grouse to eat later in the winter and gathers the lower ones to make the perfect sauce to accompany this most delicate and delicious of birds.

Unlike the more usual grain eaters, the ruffed grouse is the only gallinaceous bird who chooses to make up a large part of his autumn diet with hawthorn apples, wild grapes, wild cherries, blackberries, highbush cranberries, and apples. This feasting on fruit imparts a totally unique flavor to these noble birds.

The important period of survival for ruffed grouse is winter, when they feed on the buds of hardwoods, principally aspen, in the North. They eat quickly and in fifteen minutes can gulp enough buds to nourish themselves for the day. Then they dive into a snowbank and stay warm and safe from predators.

Viburnum trilobum is the Latin name of the domestic highbush cranberry. The shrubs can be purchased from most well-stocked nurseries, and they make a handsome as well as useful addition to the garden. If you don't have a viburnum bush, or can't find the wild ones, use regular fresh cranberries in an equal amount. The sauce will enhance turkey, pheasant, or quail, as well as grouse.

Highbush Cranberry Sauce

MAKES 1½ PINTS

4 cups of highbush cranberries, with large stems cut off and small stems cut short
2 tablespoons water
Juice of 1 lemon
Rind of 1 lemon, grated
¾ cup superfine sugar
½ teaspoon freshly grated nutmeg
½ teaspoon cinnamon

Cut the large central stems off the berries and trim the small stems to roughly ¼ inch long, thus separating the clusters of berries. Wash them under cold running water in a colander.

Place water, lemon juice, and berries in an enameled pan. Place on medium-high heat, bring to a boil, lower the heat, and simmer for 15 minutes, until the berries pop open. Stir occasionally so they don't stick to the bottom of the pan. Remove from the heat and put them through a food mill, or push through a sieve with a wooden spoon, to remove seeds and stems.

Add the sugar, cinnamon, nutmeg, and grated lemon rind. Replace on low heat and stir until sugar melts. Pour into sterilized jars and seal if you are going to store it for future use, or refrigerate and rewarm over low heat when you are ready to use it. It should not be really hot, but warmer than room temperature when you serve it.

Mushroom Pie

SERVES 6

Preheat oven to 350°.

Wash mushrooms quickly in water with a little vinegar added to it. Drain, and slice about ¼ inch thick. Sauté on medium-low heat for 8 to 10 minutes. Reserve liquid in the pan and remove mushrooms with a slotted spoon to a plate. Set aside.

Pour liquid from mushrooms into a measuring cup and fill with enough light cream to make 2 cups altogether. In a heavy-bottomed saucepan melt 2 tablespoons of butter, then add the flour, allowing it to bubble over low heat for 3 minutes. Do not let it brown.

Add the mushroom liquid and light cream combination all at once and whisk constantly for 3 to 5 minutes over medium heat, until the sauce has thickened. Remove from heat and set aside.

In a small frying pan, sauté the onions in 1 tablespoon butter until they are soft and transparent. Add to the cream sauce with the salt and pepper. Add the mushrooms and mix well. Pour into the pie shell. Cover with rolled-out pie dough and crimp the edges. Brush

2 cups sliced, sautéed mushrooms (If they're wild, so much the better.)
2 tablespoons butter
2 tablespoons flour (potato or rice flour if possible)
Liquid from mushrooms and enough light cream to make 2 cups
1 teaspoon salt
Dash white pepper
1 tablespoon finely chopped onion
1 tablespoon butter
1 egg yolk, beaten with 1 tablespoon water and pinch salt
One 8-inch unbaked pie shell and dough for top (see recipe for Onion Tart shell)

the top with the yolk-water mixture and prick in several places with a fork. Bake in the preheated oven for 45 to 50 minutes.

If you want the pie to look especially festive, cut 3 mushroom shapes out of pie dough. Arrange them on the crust top and brush with the egg-water mixture.

This pie can be made ahead and served at room temperature, or it can be frozen uncooked and baked for 1 hour on the day you want to serve it.

This is called "A Dinner for Your Dearest Friends," for reasons obvious to any Vermont ruffed grouse hunter. One does not share hard-won ruffed grouse with simply casual friends or acquaintances, however charming. Having trudged up and down the Taconic and Green Mountains for a week to get six of these delectable birds (*if* one is lucky and a superb shot to boot), it's understood that using them *all* for one dinner is a Special Occasion.

Roast Ruffed Grouse

ALLOW 1 BIRD FOR EACH 2 PEOPLE UNLESS YOU CAN AFFORD TO BE MORE GENEROUS

For hanging and cleaning instructions, see Appendix.
Preheat oven to 350°.

Place the oven-ready grouse in an open pan, breast side up, with a splash of water. Place 3 strips of bacon over the breast and put it in the preheated oven. Set a timer for 30 minutes and check the birds at the end of that time. The internal temperature is critical and should be 140° to 150° on the Thermicator. If you don't have the instrument, use a sharp knife and make a slit next to the breastbone. It should be a moist, pale pink at the center fading to white at the outer edges.

Remove from the oven and use game shears to snip it in half, cutting away the center 1½ inch of the back. Place on a heated platter, skin side up. Put the crisp bacon over the birds and garnish with big bunches of parsley or watercress at either end. Tuck a cluster of highbush cranberries into the greens and pass the warm cranberry sauce. Serve with Wild Rice (*which see*).

I recommend taking the telephone off the hook, sending the kids to Auntie Emma's, and pouring the best California chardonnay you can afford. Don't let anything or anyone interrupt you during this meal. It's one of the most memorable you'll ever eat.

Crème Brûlée

SERVES 6

This is certainly a classic dessert, and deservedly so. The rich creaminess topped with a thin, crunchy layer of caramelized sugar is irresistible. To prepare this successfully, the cream mixture should be made the day before serving and chilled overnight in the refrigerator. Caramelizing the sugar is made much easier and more professional by the use of a *salamander* or sugar iron.

1½ cups whipping cream
4 egg yolks
1 cup superfine sugar
One ½-inch vanilla bean, or 1 teaspoon vanilla extract
1 cup light brown sugar

If you can't find one, this can be done under a broiler, but it's not as much fun.

Place the cream and vanilla bean in a heavy-bottomed saucepan and warm over low heat. Beat the egg yolks with the sugar in a large bowl until they are light colored and thick. Whisk the warm cream into the eggs gradually (having removed the vanilla bean, if using one).

Return the pan to low heat and stir until the custard coats the back of the metal spoon.

Remove from the heat, mix in the vanilla (if you haven't used the vanilla bean), and pour ¼ cup of the mixture into each of 6 individual ovenproof ramekins or tempered glass custard cups, 3 inches in diameter. Chill in refrigerator overnight.

The following day cover the tops of the cream mixtures completely with light brown sugar about ¼ inch thick. Do not let any cream show around the edges.

Preheat the broiler.

Put the salamander over medium heat on top of the stove to heat up. Place the small ramekins in a large baking pan for ease of handling, and put it under the preheated broiler until the sugar starts to melt, about 2 minutes. Remove from under the broiler, and finish the caramelizing process with the heated sugar iron, pressing it down lightly on the sugar and moving it fairly rapidly over the surface of the sugar until it is all melted completely and glazed looking. (You may have to reheat the salamander once or twice.) Let cool about 3 minutes and then place ice cubes around the individual ramekins in the baking pan. Add a little cold water and chill until ready to serve. Don't put it in the refrigerator; this will soften the crisp topping. Add ice cubes as needed while it is waiting.

If you don't have a salamander, leave the crèmes under the broiler until the sugar is melted and bubbling. Remove from the heat, let cool a little, and add ice and water to the baking pan around the ramekins to keep them chilled.

THIRTY-ONE

A CLASSIC WILD DUCK DINNER

November

ROAST WILD DUCK SERVED ON BROWN BREAD WITH PRESSED
ESSENCE OF DUCK AND CURRANT-SHERRY SAUCE

◆

WILD RICE

◆

CREAMED PEARL ONIONS

◆

SPICED APPLESAUCE

◆

ROBERT MONDAVI NAPA VALLEY CABERNET SAUVIGNON

◆

FROZEN LEMON SOUFFLÉ

A Classic: The Cedar Point Club Wild Duck Dinner

From before the turn of the century until the late 1950s, this wild duck dinner was served at the Cedar Point Club on the southern shore of Lake Erie, west of Sandusky. It is a way of presenting duck that is simple, yet care must be taken in cooking the ducks. There is no thick orange sauce or flaming brandy to disguise ducks that are brown and tasteless all the way through. If a duck-eating purist sees well-done birds, he will mentally or literally relegate them to the soup pot or pâté press, depending upon whether he is host or guest. The meat should be medium pink, firm, and tender—the exact internal temperature should read 140° on the Thermicator.

Please note that this method calls for a duck press, which is available from the Orvis Company, Manchester, Vermont 05254. It isn't absolutely necessary, but you will lose some of the ritual and also the delicious juices of the duck if you don't use one. However, the duck soup you can make from the carcasses will compensate for the loss. Once you have pressed the duck, the carcasses are useless for soup, naturally. All the flavorful juices have been pressed out of them.

See the Appendix for hanging and cleaning instructions.

Allow one oven-ready mallard, black, or pintail duck for each person.

Preheat oven to 475°.

Place ducks, breast side up, in an open pan with a splash of water. Cook for 19 to 21 minutes, until the internal temperature is 140°. Check each bird with a Thermicator or with a sharp knife next to the breastbone. If the meat is reddish pink against the bone, fading to lighter pink at the outside edge, it's done. The birds do not all cook at the same rate however, due to their position in the oven, so check every bird, not just the one in the middle.

While the ducks are cooking, butter the same number of thin whole wheat bread slices on one side, halve them, and put on a serving plate.

Melt the contents of two 10-ounce jars of red currant jelly in a pan and add 4 tablespoons Tio Pepe dry sherry. Heat (do not boil) and pour into a sauce boat or pitcher and keep warm. (If you are cooking only 2 ducks, use 1 jar of currant jelly and 2 tablespoons sherry.)

Remove the ducks from the oven as they get done, fillet breasts, and place them, skin side down, on a warm platter. If you prefer, peel off the skin before serving and crisp it in a 475° oven for 15 to 20 minutes. Garnish with big bunches of parsley and kumquats or cherry tomatoes.

Now take the carcasses of the ducks and press the juice out of them in the duck press. Add the pan drippings and pour into a sauce boat or pitcher.

Arrange the bread, the two sauces, and the duck, in that order. To serve, place the bread, *buttered side down*, on the plate. On 1 half-slice, pour the duck juice, on the other half-slice pour the currant-sherry sauce. Place the duck breasts on top, skin side down.

For accompaniments you *must* serve creamed pearl onions, buttered wild rice, and spicy homemade applesauce. All of these combine to create an unforgettable melange of textures and flavors. No wonder the twelve members of this club had this menu prepared every weekend of the season! There are still some great old duck clubs in the vast marshes of this area. Unhappily, Cedar Point is no longer among them. Fortunate guests were presented with beautifully engraved gold pins (see below) that depicted a boat, closely resembling Noah's ark, which had been their first clubhouse. These are much cherished and appear on the hats of the lucky few at some retriever and field trials.

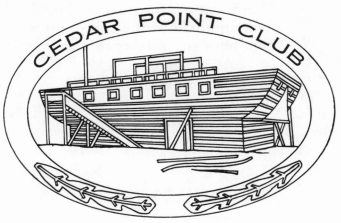

A Classic Wild Duck Dinner

Wild Rice

ALLOW ¼ CUP DRY RICE PER SERVING

Put the rice in a large saucepan, add water to cover at least 6 inches deep, and bring to a boil. Lower heat and simmer, uncovered, for 15 minutes.

Pour water and rice into a fine sieve, rinse with hot water. Return rice to pan, refill with water, and put back on heat. Bring to a boil and simmer another 15 minutes. Repeat this process once more, cooking the rice for 45 minutes in all.

After the last 15 minutes of cooking, drain the rice well, pour into a heated serving bowl, add at least 6 tablespoons of butter (cut into small pieces), and salt and pepper to taste.

Use any rice that is left over for Duck Soup (*which see*) or for Cold Wild Rice Salad (*which see*).

Creamed Pearl Onions

SERVES 8

The creamed pearl onions can be bought frozen with sauce. All they need is some freshly grated nutmeg on top. It's difficult to find fresh pearl onions in the fall and winter, and all that peeling of the tiny, slippery things can be quite a chore. Don't do it, unless you are a total purist. If you can only find plain frozen pearl onions, make a simple cream sauce to pour over them after they are cooked.

3 cups fresh or frozen pearl onions, boiled and drained

4 tablespoons butter

4 tablespoons flour (potato or rice flour is best)

2 cups milk or thin cream, scalded with 1 small bay leaf, 2 thin slices of onion, 2 sprigs of parsley, and 1 whole clove

1 teaspoon freshly grated nutmeg

Melt the butter in a heavy saucepan. Add the flour and whisk until flour is incorporated into the butter. Let the flour bubble gently for 3 minutes over low heat. Do not let it brown. Have the scalded milk or cream ready, strain the bay leaf and other seasonings out of it, and pour it into the butter-flour mixture and whisk continuously for approximately 3 to 4 minutes, until sauce is thickened.

You can make this up to a week ahead of time and keep it in a jar in the refrigerator. Reheat it in the top of a double boiler, add the boiled, drained onions, and grate 1 teaspoon fresh nutmeg over the top before serving. Add salt and pepper to taste.

Spiced Applesauce

SERVES 8

Wash and quarter the apples and pears. Place in a heavy saucepan with the lemon juice, grated rind, and 2 or 3 tablespoons of water. Keep the heat low and stir from time to time so the apples don't stick or burn. When apples are soft (approximately 15 minutes), remove from heat, and pass through a food mill or a sieve. Add the cinnamon, nutmeg, and sugar to taste. (Some apples are more tart than others—start with ½ cup sugar and add more if desired.)

This can be made weeks ahead of time and frozen, or kept in the refrigerator for a week. Reheat it over very low heat before serving.

Use any leftover applesauce to make very easy and delicious Applesauce Tarts (*which see*) for dessert at another meal.

6 Granny Smith apples
2 ripe pears
½ cup sugar
1 teaspoon cinnamon
½ teaspoon freshly grated
    nutmeg
Grated rind of 1 lemon
Juice of 1 lemon

Frozen Lemon Soufflé

SERVES 6 TO 8 AMPLY

This dessert should have at least 4 hours to freeze. You can make it several days in advance and keep it in the freezer until ready to serve.

Prepare a 5-cup soufflé dish with a parchment paper collar fastened on the outside with a rubber band. The collar should extend above the rim of the dish by at least 4 inches.

Combine yolks and 1½ cups sugar (reserve ¼ cup) in a copper bowl, and beat over low heat until light and lemon-colored. Add lemon juice and beat until thick and very foamy. Add lemon rind, mix thoroughly, and pour into a large bowl. Cool.

Whip cream until stiff, add 1 tablespoon sugar, whip

12 egg yolks
1¾ cups sugar
¾ cup lemon juice
Grated rind of 5 lemons
½ cup heavy cream
6 egg whites
½ cup extra whipped cream
    (optional)
Candied rose or violet petals
    (optional)

to mix in sugar, and set aside. Beat the egg whites until lightly stiff, add remaining sugar, and beat until very stiff. Fold cream into egg-lemon mixture.

Fold a small amount of the egg whites into the lemon mixture, then reverse and pour the entire lemon mixture over the whites and fold in carefully. Leave some small pieces of white showing, it's better than over-folding.

Pour into prepared soufflé dish, smooth top gently, and freeze at least 4 hours. Serve directly from freezer to table.

Optional: Remove the soufflé when it's frozen hard and pipe whipped cream around the edges. Decorate it with candied rose or violet petals. Return it to the freezer and serve it directly from there.

If you are going to keep this in the freezer longer than a few hours, let it freeze solid and wrap it with foil or plastic wrap to protect it from freezer burn. Remove this covering the instant you remove the soufflé from the freezer so it won't stick and ruin your decorations.

This is a very lemony and light-tasting dessert, and it goes down very well after the heartier flavors of the duck dinner.

THIRTY-TWO

HUNTER'S LUNCHEON

November

DUCK SOUP

◆

MOLDED AVOCADO MOUSSE WITH SHRIMP AND MUSTARD
MAYONNAISE SAUCE

◆

FRESH FRUIT COMPOTE

◆

BUTTERSCOTCH BROWNIES

Duck Soup

This recipe is intended to use the duck remaining after the breasts have been filleted for a duck dinner. Any number of carcasses can be used, simply adjust the seasonings for a larger batch of soup. Admittedly, it is a messy job to bone the duck after it has been boiled, but it goes quickly because the meat is falling off the bones anyway. It's all worth it for this hearty, soul-satisfying soup, which is a meal in itself.

4 duck carcasses (fillets removed)

Add water to cover in a large pan, bring to a boil, and simmer 2½ hours. Cool. Strip meat from bones, discard skin and bones. Skim off most of the fat. (This is easier if you refrigerate the broth and meat at this point. The fat rises and hardens on the surface, making it easy to lift off and discard.)

Return broth and meat to the heat. Add remaining ingredients except sherry and rice (or barley).

4 diced carrots

3 medium-sized yellow onions, diced

6 stalks celery, diced (including leafy tops)

1½ teaspoons marjoram

1½ teaspoons thyme

1 teaspoon oregano

1 bay leaf

Very dry sherry, 1 ounce per serving

4 cups wild rice or barley, cooked

Bring broth, meat, vegetables, and seasonings to a boil and simmer 20 minutes. Add salt and pepper to taste. Add the 4 cups *cooked* wild rice or barley, simmer 10 more minutes, and remove bay leaf. Warm the soup bowls, pour an ounce of sherry into each, fill with the soup, and serve.

Do not attempt to cook the wild rice or barley in the duck broth. They must be cooked separately.

Molded Avocado Mousse with Shrimp

SERVES 8

A smooth, mild-tasting avocado mousse goes well following the robust soup. Serve it with a crusty bread or hard rolls.

Warm ½ cup of the stock in a small pan and dissolve gelatin in it, stirring constantly. Combine all ingredients except the shrimp in a food processor or blender and run until the avocado is puréed. Pour into an oiled ring mold that has been rinsed with cold water and the excess water shaken out, and chill in the refrigerator for at least 3 hours.

At serving time, dip the mold into hot water for 4 seconds, wipe the water off the outside of the mold, and place the serving plate on top of the mold. Invert and lift the mold off.

Fill the center of the ring with the cooked shrimp and place small lettuce leaves or watercress around the outside edge. Serve with Mustard Mayonnaise Sauce.

If you haven't time to make the mayonnaise, add 1 tablespoon fresh lime or lemon juice and a little grated rind to each cup of the least-sweet commercial mayonnaise you can buy.

2 large ripe avocados, peeled, halved, and seeded
½ teaspoon onion juice
½ cup sour cream
½ cup half-and-half
Salt and pepper to taste
1 cup chicken consommé or good chicken stock
1 packet unflavored gelatin
2 pounds cooked shrimp

Mustard Mayonnaise Sauce

SERVES ABOUT 8

Put everything except the oil into a blender or food processor, and add the oil very slowly in a steady stream while processing. It will thicken almost immediately. Serve in a sauce boat next to the salad.

1 egg at room temperature (Put eggs in warm water for 10 minutes if you haven't removed them from the refrigerator in time.)
1 teaspoon prepared Dijon mustard
¼ teaspoon garlic salt
Salt and freshly ground pepper to taste
2 tablespoons vinegar
1 cup light olive oil or salad oil

For dessert, use any combination of fresh fruit in season. Peel and cut up into a glass bowl. Pour a few tablespoons of brandy, calvados, or Cointreau over it and chill. Serve the fruit with Butterscotch Brownies or Green Pepper Cookies (*which see*).

Butterscotch Brownies

YIELDS ABOUT 12 LARGE BROWNIES

½ cup melted butter
2 eggs
1 teaspoon baking powder
1 teaspoon vanilla extract
2 cups brown sugar
½ teaspoon salt
1½ cups flour
1 cup chopped walnuts

Preheat oven to 350°.

Cream butter, eggs, and brown sugar together. Sift baking powder, salt, and flour over the butter mixture and combine well. Add the vanilla and walnuts, stir to mix in thoroughly, and turn into a greased 8 × 13-inch pan.

Bake 25 minutes in the preheated oven. Remove, allow to cool slightly, and cut into squares.

You can skip the fruit and serve the brownies with vanilla ice cream and butterscotch sauce if the hunters are teenage boys who have been walk-shooting all morning.

THIRTY-THREE

A PLANTATION THANKSGIVING

November

CAVIAR MOUSSE

◆

MOET AND CHANDON BRUT IMPERIAL CHAMPAGNE

◆

ROAST WILD TURKEY WITH STUFFING

◆

CREAMED PURÉE OF SQUASH, LEEK, AND CARROT

◆

HIGHBUSH CRANBERRY SAUCE

◆

SPINACH GRATINÉE

◆

BOSTON LETTUCE SALAD WITH CREAMY MUSTARD DRESSING

◆

BUTTERMILK BISCUITS WITH TUPELO HONEY OR PRESERVES

◆

PLANTATION PERSIMMON PUDDING

Caviar Mousse

MAKES ONE 3-CUP MOLD

1 tablespoon unflavored gelatin
¼ cup cold water
1 tablespoon lemon juice
Grated rind of 1 lemon
1 tablespoon Worcestershire
    sauce
2 tablespoons mayonnaise
1 pint sour cream
Pinch dry mustard
¼ cup chopped parsley
2 tablespoons finely chopped
    onion
One 4-ounce jar black caviar
    (Please don't use Beluga for
    this recipe.)
4 hard-boiled eggs

Sauté the finely chopped onion in 1 tablespoon butter and cook until soft, not browned. Set aside to cool.

Dissolve the gelatin in the cold water, and when dissolved heat very gently in a small saucepan for 1 minute to completely dissolve it. Pour into a large bowl and add the mayonnaise, mustard, parsley, onion, Worcestershire, lemon juice, and grated rind. Mix thoroughly. Fold in the sour cream and caviar. Add salt and pepper to taste, if desired, and place in a 3-cup mold and chill in the refrigerator for at least 6 hours. Or, you can make small individual mousses and serve this as a first course at a sit-down dinner.

Unmold and place on a chilled serving platter. Garnish around the bottom with quartered hard-boiled eggs. Add a few sprigs of parsley for color and serve with melba toast, fresh buttered toast points, or freshly baked white Brittle Bread (which see).

It really is too bad that the wild turkey isn't our national emblem. He barely resembles the fat, stupid domestic turkey. The wild one is lean and smart. He's sensitive, strong, and dignified. He doesn't prey on other species. He likes to live in vast climax forests.

The state game commission introduced thirty-one turkeys from western New York State into Vermont in 1969. The turkeys had to be captured one at a time (no mean feat) and immediately put on a plane and flown to their new location and released. A wild turkey will not live in captivity for more than five or six hours.

Wild turkeys had been wiped out of Vermont one hundred years ago when all the forests were cut for pasture and farmland. Following the Civil War, Vermont veterans came home, packed up the family and all their belongings, and abandoned the state for greener (and less rocky) pastures down South.

The forests grew up, and one hundred years later again became the perfect habitat for wild turkeys. There are now over twenty thousand of them in Vermont. The program was wildly successful (forgive the pun).

We freeze the spring gobbler from Vermont and around Thanksgiving time take it down South for a plantation feast.

Roast Wild Turkey

See Appendix for instruction on cleaning and hanging.

Preheat oven to 350°.

Weigh the oven-ready bird and multiply the dressed weight by 12. Example: If it's a 12-pound turkey, it will take approximately 144 minutes, or 2 hours and 24 minutes, to cook.

Place the bird in a shallow roasting pan with enough strips of bacon to cover the breast. Roast in the pre-heated oven for the allotted time. Test with the Thermicator. The meat should be between 140° and 150° internal temperature. If you don't have a Thermicator, make a slit with a sharp knife next to the breastbone. Peer into the slit while holding it open with the knife. If the meat is still red at the center, return the turkey to the oven for 15 minutes and check again at the end of that time. The center should be pink.

It is important to remove the bird from the oven when it reaches 150°. It should rest for 10 or 15 minutes before carving, and it will continue to cook during that period. The meat will be moist and have a distinctive flavor not found in domestic turkey. Don't lose it by overcooking. A turkey is one bird that is large enough to stuff without danger of overcooking the meat in order to properly cook the stuffing.

Be sure before using the turkey gizzard that it has been cut open and rinsed thoroughly under cold, running water. Remove the inner lining before proceeding to use it with the heart and liver.

A Plantation Thanksgiving

Turkey Stuffing

1 loaf good white bread, stale
2 eggs
¾ cup diced celery
½ cup diced onion
2 teaspoons rosemary,
   crumbled
¼ cup chopped parsley
2 teaspoons salt
Freshly ground pepper
Cooked giblets and reserved
   broth
1 cup (2 sticks) butter

Put the neck and giblets of the turkey in a saucepan, add 1½ cups water and the tops of 3 celery stalks. Simmer on low heat for 30 minutes. Reserve the broth. Discard the neck and celery leaves and put the giblets through a food processor or a hand grinder. Place in a large bowl and set aside.

Crumble or cube the bread. Melt the butter in a large frying pan, add the onion and celery, and cook until the onions take on a golden color. Stir into the bread crumbs, then add the parsley, rosemary, eggs, puréed giblets, and salt and pepper. Add enough of the reserved broth to moisten. Mix well, taste for seasoning, and adjust if necessary.

Optional additions are: 1 pint oysters in their liquor, or 2 cups pecans, roughly chopped. If using the oysters, drain the liquor from them and place it in a saucepan. Heat to the boiling point, cut the oysters in half if they are large, add to the hot liquid, and cook until the edges begin to curl. Stir into the stuffing.

Stuff the breast cavity loosely with the dressing and bake the turkey for the length of time you have figured for its weight.

Creamed Purée of Squash, Leek, and Carrot

SERVES 10 TO 12

Preheat oven to 350°.

Halve the acorn squash. If using a larger squash, cut it in quarters or sixths. Remove seeds and put in a shallow ovenproof dish or pan, cut side down. Bake for 35 to 40 minutes. Remove from the oven, cool, and scoop cooked squash from the skin. Melt 2 tablespoons of butter in 2 tablespoons oil in a large frying pan, and put the squash pulp into it. Cook, stirring occasionally, on low heat for 10 to 15 minutes, until all liquid has evaporated. Do not brown. Remove to the bowl of a food processor or blender and purée.

Melt another 2 tablespoons butter in 2 tablespoons of oil in the same pan and place the carrots, cut roughly into rounds, and the roughly chopped leeks into it. After the first 5 minutes of cooking, add just enough chicken broth to keep the vegetables from sticking, cover, and cook another 15 minutes, stirring occasionally, until the carrots are soft. Put the cooked leeks and carrots through the food processor or a food mill. Place all the puréed vegetables into the frying pan, add ½ cup heavy cream, and salt and pepper to taste. Cook for 5 minutes on low to heat through, mixing well.

Serve in a deep bowl and garnish with a few sprigs of parsley. This recipe can be made ahead of time and reheated in a double boiler on top of the stove, or in a soufflé dish or casserole set in a roasting pan of boiling water and heated in a 350° oven. It will take 15 to 20 minutes. Stir it occasionally while it is reheating.

The recipe for Highbush Cranberry Sauce can be found in Chapter 30.

¼ cup butter (½ stick)
3 leeks (white part only), halved lengthwise and diced
1 large butternut squash (about 3 pounds), or 6 acorn squash
10 carrots
½ cup chicken stock (Canned broth is all right.)
½ cup heavy cream
2 tablespoons salt
Freshly ground pepper
4 tablespoons oil

Spinach Gratinée

4 cups cooked chopped spinach,
   or 4 packages frozen chopped
   spinach
1 teaspoon freshly grated
   nutmeg to taste
1½ cups freshly grated
   Parmesan cheese
4 tablespoons butter
4 tablespoons flour (potato or
   rice flour is best)
1 cup milk
1 cup heavy cream
1 slice onion
1 bay leaf
1 sprig fresh tarragon, or ½
   teaspoon dried tarragon
3 sprigs fresh parsley, or ½
   teaspoon dried parsley
1 teaspoon salt
5 peppercorns

Put the spinach on low heat in a heavy frying pan and let it cook until the liquid is completely evaporated. Stir it occasionally. Pour the milk and cream into a heavy saucepan. Add the onion, bay leaf, tarragon, peppercorns, and parsley. Bring to a boil and let simmer gently for 5 minutes.

Melt the butter in another heavy saucepan. Add the flour and let bubble for 3 minutes. Add the milk-cream mixture through a strainer, discard the herbs, and whisk constantly until mixture is thick and smooth. Add salt to taste and simmer gently for 2 to 3 minutes. Remove from heat and stir in ¾ cup of the grated Parmesan cheese, reserving ¾ cup. Add the nutmeg, mix thoroughly, and line the bottom of a buttered oval au gratin pan or other ovenproof baking dish with half the cream sauce. Arrange the spinach on top. Spread the remaining half of the sauce over the spinach and sprinkle the reserved cheese on top.

Place under the broiler until the cheese is melted and the top is lightly browned, about 5 minutes. Serve at once.

Boston Lettuce with Creamy Mustard Dressing

SERVES 10 TO 12

Whisk the mustard, vinegar, egg yolk, Worcestershire sauce, lemon juice and Tabasco together. Add the oil gradually while whisking constantly. Add the heavy cream, and salt and pepper, and whisk until well mixed. Pour over chilled Boston lettuce and serve immediately.

4 large heads Boston lettuce, washed, dried, torn, and chilled
4 tablespoons prepared Dijon mustard
4 tablespoons red wine vinegar
2 raw egg yolks
½ teaspoon Worcestershire sauce
Dash Tabasco sauce
¾ cup oil
Salt and freshly ground pepper to taste
4 tablespoons heavy cream
2 teaspoons lemon juice

Buttermilk Biscuits

MAKES 12 TO 15 BISCUITS

Preheat oven to 425°.

Sift flour, baking soda, baking powder, and salt together into a bowl. Add buttermilk and blend with a fork until you have a soft dough. Place on a lightly floured board and roll to ½ inch thick.

Cut biscuits with a small biscuit cutter or glass dipped in flour. Place on a greased cookie sheet and bake in the preheated oven for 12 to 15 minutes. They should be golden brown on top.

Serve hot with butter and honey. Tupelo honey is available from the Orvis Company. It has an intriguing smoky taste and is the one honey that will not crystallize, ever.

2 cups sifted all-purpose flour
1 teaspoon baking soda
1 teaspoon baking powder
1 teaspoon salt
1 cup buttermilk

Plantation Persimmon Pudding

2 tablespoons butter, softened
4 tablespoons butter, melted
2 cups unsifted flour
2 teaspoons baking soda
1 teaspoon ground cinnamon
1 teaspoon ground ginger
½ teaspoon freshly ground
   nutmeg
2 pounds ripe persimmons
2 cups sugar
1 cup milk
1 cup seedless golden raisins
2 teaspoons vanilla extract
1 cup heavy cream, whipped

Preheat oven to 350°. Butter two 1-quart soufflé dishes.

The persimmons have to be ripe. They should "shake like jelly on a plate," as the song goes. If they are ripe enough, the stems will pull out with the white membrane attached.

Pull out the stems and membrane and cut in half. Seed them if they have seeds—some have none. Cut out any dark spots in the skin, otherwise leave the skin on, and purée in a food processor or blender.

Add the sugar and run the machine for a few seconds to blend it thoroughly. You should have 1 cup of purée. Place it in a large bowl.

Sift together the flour, baking soda, and spices, and add to the purée alternately with the milk. Add the melted butter, vanilla, and raisins.

Pour into 2 buttered 1-quart soufflé dishes and bake 50 to 60 minutes, until it shrinks away from the sides of the dish. Allow the pudding to cool at least 15 minutes before serving. It's just as good after it cools to room temperature. Cut into wedges and place some whipped cream on each serving.

If you ever find enough wild persimmons to make this recipe or the ice cream in Chapter 3, by all means try to do it. Either dish would be supreme, even though making them this way would entail seeding an enormous number of those walnut-sized little fruits. If I ever find enough to do it, I will. I understand that there are scads of wild persimmons in Indiana.

THIRTY-FOUR

THE ANNUAL DUCK SHOOT AND DOGFIGHT

November

STREAKERS

◆

CHEESE STRATA

◆

COUNTRY SAUSAGE

◆

BUTTERED STONEGROUND GRITS

◆

SAUTÉED CHERRY TOMATOES

◆

SAUTÉED MUSHROOMS

◆

FIVE GRAIN TOAST, BISCUITS, TOASTED ENGLISH MUFFINS

◆

ASSORTED HONEY, JAMS, AND JELLIES

In the Monticello, Florida, area the duck season usually opens on Thanksgiving Day. Leigh's two Georgia-based sisters and their families join us for the opening duck shoot on or about 27 November, which is also Leigh's birthday.

Having a triple motivation to get together, we rise at four-thirty or five in the morning and meet near our Big Duck Pond 45 minutes before sunrise. Everyone drives in with the headlights off, so as not to alert the ducks. As many as eighteen people quietly get out of their vehicles in utter blackness. They whisper greetings and draw lots for their blinds.

When the hunters open the back hatches of the various jeeps and station wagons to get out their shotguns, six to twelve black Labs also pour out into the complete darkness—and immediately accost one another. In the pitch black, it's very difficult to know which dog is battling which. The melee is quickly stopped by the dog handler and various owners, and the party, breaking up into pairs, drags their respective beasts to the assigned blinds.

No matter how many leashes, dog crates, or wire guards are introduced from year to year to keep order, there is always some point in the morning's proceedings at which Tara (Sallie's dog) decides she hates Hannah (our dog), or Twinkle (Kate's dog) moves to take a piece out of Alfie (Gert's dog). It's all part of the Holiday Ritual, and we have learned to take it philosophically. We even wear teeshirts now, depicting each plantation family as the "Mays Pond Maulers," the "Beverly Bashers," and the "Borderline Beasts."

Around nine o'clock, after the shoot, everyone loads up the dogs, guns, and ducks, and goes to the house for a well-deserved breakfast. Since the hostess (and cook) has also been out shooting, the menu calls for dishes that can be prepared ahead of time, or put in the oven with the timer set to go at eight o'clock.

The stoneground grits have been cooked the requisite 45 minutes the evening before. They will be in a double boiler, ready to be heated with a little cream and butter added.

The tomatoes and mushrooms are halved or quartered, ready to sauté quickly on top of the stove while the various breads are being toasted or warmed.

The sausage, in large links, is in the oven with the egg dish, which was prepared the evening before. All that is needed is two or three people who are handy with oyster knives and it's ready to roll.

The regional Apalachicola oysters are the best in the world as far as we're concerned. In fact, we added an oyster bar onto the kitchen because we consume about fifty dozen oysters a week when we have a full house.

The idea of oysters for breakfast may put a few fainthearted souls off, but cooked ones are different. They are a delicious first course for any meal, and people who would never touch a raw oyster become inordinately fond of them when they are prepared as Streakers.

Streakers

ALLOW 6 OYSTERS ON THE HALF SHELL PER SERVING

Put the opened oysters in their shells on a jelly roll pan or cookie sheet with a rolled edge to avoid the juices running off all over the oven or you or the floor.

SAUCE

Shake all the sauce ingredients together in a pint jar and spoon it over the opened oysters, being sure to put some garlic particles on each oyster. Place a small piece of raw bacon on each oyster and broil on the top shelf of the oven for about 4 or 5 minutes, until the oysters are curled at the edges and the bacon is crisp. Watch them carefully, the bacon burns very quickly.

Serve on oyster plates. (If you have time to transfer them before everyone gathers around with oyster forks in hand and eats them all right off the cooking pan.)

One could be happy eating a dozen or so of these with a nice green salad and crusty bread for a luncheon or a light supper.

FOR ABOUT 60 OYSTERS

*5 garlic cloves, peeled and put
   through a garlic press*
½ cup fresh lemon juice
*1 tablespoon Worcestershire
   sauce*
*Tabasco sauce to taste (¼
   teaspoon is recommended,
   unless you're from Louisiana
   or Texas)*
60 small pieces of raw bacon

Cheese Strata

9 *slices good white bread,*
crusts removed, cut into ½-
inch cubes

1½ *tablespoons finely minced*
onion

1 *pound sharp cheddar cheese,*
shredded, or cut into very
small dice

3 *eggs*

3 *cups of milk*

1 *tablespoon each Dijon*
mustard and Worcestershire
sauce

½ *teaspoon each salt and*
pepper

1 *cup cubed cooked ham*

This dish *must* be prepared the evening before and refrigerated until you are ready to cook it next day.

Butter a 2-quart baking dish. Layer bread, onion, cheese, and the ham in the casserole. Beat the eggs, milk, and seasonings together. Pour over the bread mixture. Cover with foil or plastic wrap and let stand overnight in the refrigerator.

Preheat oven to 300°. Bake for 1 hour, or until puffed with the center set.

This is also a perfect brunch or luncheon dish. It's old-fashioned and wholesome. It's also much easier than scrambling 2 or 3 dozen eggs at the last minute.

To order the best stoneground grits and whole-hog sausage, write: Bradley's Country Store, Centerville Road, Miccosukee, Florida 32309. They mail these items all over the country to devoted grit-and-sausage lovers. Ask for large-link mild sausages or large-link hot sausages. The grits come in 1-pound bags. Don't order less than 10 pounds of sausage, or you will only have to reorder the next day after you try them. There are 4 links to the pound.

THIRTY-FIVE

A PLANTATION PICNIC
FOR QUAIL HUNTERS

December

CONSOMMÉ SENEGALESE

◆

TIO PEPE DRY SHERRY

◆

CHARCOAL-GRILLED QUAIL

◆

WILD RICE SALAD

◆

COLD BRUSSELS SPROUTS VINAIGRETTE

◆

ASSORTED OLIVES AND CRUDITÉS

◆

DEVILED GAME HEN EGGS

◆

CUCUMBER AND TOMATO SANDWICHES
ON HOMEMADE BREAD

◆

COLD PERSIMMON PUDDING

◆

POTATO CHIP COOKIES

In the South, quail can be hunted in three ways: walk-shooting with a Brittany Spaniel who both points and retrieves the birds; on horseback with an English Setter running ahead (with one in reserve parked in the shade nearby); or in a shooting buggy drawn by a pair of matched mules handled by a mule driver. A brace of English Pointers range out in front, followed by two or three men on horseback. The buggy follows, carrying the shooters, guns, one or two Brittanys or Labs to retrieve, six relief Pointers, extra cartridges, foul-weather gear, a tool kit, a first-aid kit, and a tank of water for the dogs built in under the dog boxes.

The Pointers are trained to be steady to wing and shot. Once they have pointed, they freeze in place and do not move a muscle until the dog handler taps them on the head, which means, "OK, you can go now." A dog may have to hold a point for half an hour or more while the shooting party is walking in on the other dog's point, shooting, and picking up the birds.

At most times, the dogs and dog handler are quite a distance in front of the buggy. The dog handler signals the mule driver that there is a point by raising his hat and holding it over his head. The buggy surges forward and two guns dismount from the buggy and walk in past the dog on either side of the dog handler, who beats the bush with his quirt.

After the convey rises and the shooting is over, the dog handler calls for a retrieving dog to come in and pick up the birds. The retriever will have seen everything that took place. He will have mentally marked the birds down and will race in and pick them up, or will find their trail, sniff them out, and bring them back to the handler's hand. Then everyone gets back on the horses or into the wagon and proceeds on the course.

Having started at 9:00 A.M., by 1:00 P.M. this entourage can be quite some distance from the house. So, depending on the course chosen or the weather forecasts, the buggy will be carrying, in addition to the aforementioned items, a picnic lunch for 6 to 10 people, to be eaten in the field.

This luncheon is a sit-down meal with a tablecloth, real plates, knives and forks, and all the usual amenities of civilized dining. A picnic table has been placed in advance overlooking a pretty part of a swamp, or with a view of a pond or lake. It doesn't have to be a hurried meal because the quail are usually inactive and are not out feeding during the heat of midday. There's even time for a little nap after luncheon is over. A fire is built and everyone relaxes until the coals are just right to grill the quail.

The cucumber and tomato sandwiches and the crudités are passed with the soup while the fire is burning down to glowing coals.

Consommé Senegalese

Mix the consommé and the curry powder together and heat to the boiling point. Simmer for 5 minutes. Remove from the heat and whisk in the cream. Pour into a thermos to keep hot, or chill and serve cold. Serve in enameled picnic cups or colorful plastic mugs. This is a surefire restorative taken with a nip of dry sherry.

1 can of chicken consommé for each 2 people (One doesn't have time to make consommé from scratch between breakfast and 9 A.M.)
½ teaspoon curry powder for each can of consommé
1 tablespoon heavy cream for each can of consommé

Charcoal-Grilled Quail

Split the quail up the breast with the game shears, or do this before you pack them. (Usually we take frozen birds that thaw out just in time for lunch, so we split them in the field. The meat lies flatter and will cook much more quickly if the birds are split through the breast instead of the back.)

Melt the butter in the frying pan on the edge of the fire. Dip the birds into the butter and place them on the grill. Cook for 3 to 4 minutes on each side. (They should be pale pink inside, fading to white on the outside edge if you make an exploratory slash alongside the breastbone.) Salt and pepper them and serve with Wild Rice Salad and Cold Brussels Sprouts Vinaigrette. Garnish each plate with 1 or 2 deviled eggs.

Allow 2 quail per serving (see Appendix for instructions on cleaning and hanging)
1 tablespoon butter for each quail
Salt and pepper
Small frying pan
Game shears

A Plantation for Quail Hunters

209

Wild Rice Salad

2 cups cooked wild rice, cooled
½ cup homemade Garlic
  Mayonnaise (which see) or ¼
  cup commercial mayonnaise
  combined with ¼ cup sour
  cream or plain yogurt
½ cup finely diced fresh green
  bell pepper
¼ cup finely diced scallions
¼ cup finely diced celery
1 tablespoon Worcestershire
  sauce
Dash Tabasco sauce
½ teaspoon garlic salt
1 teaspoon celery salt
½ teaspoon onion salt
Freshly ground pepper
Strips of red and green bell
  pepper for garnish

Put all the diced vegetables into a large bowl with the wild rice. Mix the mayonnaise with the remaining ingredients, whisk well, and pour over the rice. Combine thoroughly, taste for seasoning, and chill. Garnish the top with red and green pepper strips arranged in a row.

This recipe can be doubled or multiplied a hundredfold. I have made Wild Rice Salad for 300, which was served at the opening of the Orvis New York store.

On occasions when you are serving the salad at home or are transporting it in something other than a mule wagon (which rolls over fallen trees occasionally), garnish it with a tomato rose or two. Using a grapefruit knife, peel a small tomato carefully, trying to get just the skin and a little pulp. Keep the strip roughly ½ inch wide and all in one piece. Start with one end of the strip and roll tightly at first, more loosely on the last turn or two. Push the center up with your finger from the bottom as you slowly roll up the strip like a pinwheel. Place firmly in the rice so that it doesn't unwind after you release your grip. Cut small elliptical shapes of green pepper and place them on either side of the rose to represent leaves.

Cold Brussels Sprouts Vinaigrette

SERVES 4 TO 6

Simmer the sprouts 6 or 7 minutes, depending on size. They should still be firm and crunchy. Cool.

Mix the remaining ingredients in a medium bowl and whisk well. Pour over the sprouts and chopped vegetables and marinate in the refrigerator for 2 to 3 hours, or overnight.

There is a recipe for Hot Brussels Sprouts Vinaigrette (*which see*), but cold ones taste very different. They are much easier to take on a picnic than a salad involving lettuce or greens because they retain their crispness and texture, even at room (or air) temperature.

1 pound brussels sprouts (as small as you can find them)
¼ cup oil
1½ tablespoons lemon juice
1 teaspoon prepared Dijon mustard
2 garlic cloves, put through a garlic press
3 scallions, finely chopped
1 green bell pepper, finely chopped
1 tablespoon Worcestershire sauce
Salt and freshly ground pepper to taste

Deviled Game Hen Eggs

We happen to have a few thousand game hens because we grow them for their feathers (for fly tying). Their eggs are delicious and very appealing because they are just about half the size of a regular chicken egg. Don't worry about the size, chicken eggs will do just as well for deviled eggs. Be sure to season the mayonnaise you use to moisten the yolks with Dijon mustard, Worcestershire sauce, and a dash of Tabasco. Put a tiny sprig (1 leaf) of parsley on each egg to garnish. Pack them tightly into a quiche dish that has a paper towel spread on the bottom so they won't slide around. Cover with plastic wrap or foil and chill.

Plantation Persimmon Pudding

The recipe for Plantation Persimmon Pudding is in Chapter 33. Allow it to cool in the baking dish, cover with foil, and pack in the picnic basket.

Potato Chip Cookies

MAKES ABOUT 7 DOZEN

1 cup butter (2 sticks), very soft
1¾ cups all-purpose flour
¾ cup sugar
1 teaspoon vanilla extract
1½ ounces potato chips,
    crushed
Powdered sugar (optional)

Preheat oven to 350°.

Beat butter in a mixing bowl until light colored and very creamy. Gradually add the flour, sugar, and vanilla, mixing thoroughly. Stir in the crushed potato chips.

Drop by teaspoons onto cookie sheets and bake until lightly browned, 8 to 10 minutes. Let cool on waxed paper or paper towels. Sprinkle with powdered sugar, if desired. Try them both ways. I like them without the sugar better. They taste very much like the pecan puffs everybody makes, but they're easier and cheaper to produce.

After this meal, it's best to take a little nap before getting back on your horse.

THIRTY-SIX

A CHRISTMASTIME COCKTAIL PARTY FOR A SMALL GROUP

December

QUAIL LIVER PÂTÉ

◆

BRITTLE BREAD

◆

WOODCOCK LEGS SAUTÉED IN GARLIC BUTTER

◆

DOVE BREASTS WRAPPED IN BACON

◆

PHEASANT PÂTÉ

◆

ASSORTED CRACKERS OR TOAST POINTS

◆

"WOODS EDGE" CAVIAR AND EGG RING

◆

COCKTAIL PISSALADETTES

◆

CUVÉE DOM PERIGNON CHAMPAGNE 1978 OR SCHRAMSBERG
NAPA VALLEY RESERVE 1978

Quail Liver Pâté

One can be sure that very few people have had the pleasure of eating this rare and savory delicacy.

When cleaning and plucking quail save the livers and hearts, even though they are tiny. Freeze them in a plastic container and add to them until you have amassed ½ cup with which to prepare this recipe for a special holiday party. This can be made with duck or chicken livers also. This recipe makes 1 small mold or 2 molds the size of small custard cups.

Sauté the livers and hearts in 2 tablespoons butter over low heat for 5 minutes, stirring frequently. Remove to a plate and cool. Add 1 tablespoon butter to the same pan and sauté the minced shallot until it is transparent and soft, about 4 to 5 minutes. Add the shallot to the livers and purée them in a food processor or food mill, or push them through a fine sieve with a wooden spoon.

Resoften the gelatin again by stirring in a small amount of the liver purée, and add to the rest of the liver purée with the sour cream and mayonnaise. Add salt and freshly ground pepper to taste and mix well.

Rinse a small mold or 2 or 3 tempered glass custard cups in cold water and shake to remove the excess water. Pour the liver mixture into the mold and refrigerate for at least 3 hours. Unmold by briefly dipping into hot water and inverting onto a plate. Garnish with a sprig or two of holly and serve with piping hot Brittle Bread.

½ cup quail livers and hearts
½ packet unflavored gelatin, softened in 1 tablespoon cold water
1 small shallot, minced finely
1 tablespoon sour cream
1 tablespoon mayonnaise
3 tablespoons butter
Salt and freshly ground pepper to taste

214

Brittle Bread

Pour warm water into a large bowl, sprinkle in the yeast, and stir until thoroughly dissolved. Add sugar, salt, and ¼ pound melted butter and whisk until sugar and salt are dissolved. Add 2 cups flour and beat until smooth.

Add an additional 2 cups flour and mix to make a stiff dough. Divide into 2 batches and run each in a food processor (with a steel blade) for 3 minutes, or knead for 8 to 10 minutes by hand. Form into 1 large ball and place in a buttered bowl, rolling the dough around to coat it with butter. Cover with a clean tea towel and let rise in a warm place until doubled in bulk, about 1 hour.

Preheat oven to 350°.

Punch down and divide the dough into equal pieces. Take 1 piece at a time and pat into a rectangle. Wipe the counter or table with a damp sponge and stick an 18-inch-long piece of waxed paper onto it. Lightly flour the paper and the rolling pin. Roll out the dough into a roughly shaped rectangle 10 × 14 inches (just so it fits on a cookie sheet). Make it as thin as you can, and no thicker than ¼ inch. Place on an ungreased cookie sheet and bake for 8 minutes.

Melt the ½ stick butter. Remove the bread from the oven or just reach in, if you can do it without scorching yourself, and brush melted butter over the entire surface of the bread. Return to the oven quickly and bake until golden brown, about 5 to 6 minutes more.

Bake each of the 4 sheets of bread in the same fashion. If you have 2 cookie sheets, you can roll the next one out and have it ready to slide in the oven as you remove the first one.

This bread should be served immediately after it is removed from the oven—in 1 piece. Slide it onto a silver tray or a large board and let the guests break off whatever they want. It's good just plain, but it will go with any mousse, pâté, or dip.

It can be broken and stored in a tin with a tight-fitting lid. Or, you can roll it up uncooked in the lightly floured waxed paper and then in foil and freeze it. Thaw

1 packet dry yeast
1 cup warm water
¼ pound butter, melted, plus ½ stick butter, melted
1½ teaspoons salt
1 teaspoon sugar
4 cups all-purpose flour

completely, unroll, peel off the waxed paper, and pop into the oven whenever you need it.

Note: This dough is very elastic, it may be easier to use the rolling pin in a motion going away from your body. Lift the dough and turn it on the waxed paper to roll evenly into a rough rectangle.

This buttery, crisp bread was served to me in Savannah, Georgia, years ago and I have been mixing up terrible combinations of flour, water, and butter ever since, trying to approximate it. I believe the recipe was A Designated Regional Treasure of the South and no Damnyankee was going to get it. This is very close to the original; the mists of time have not dimmed my first impression of it.

Woodcock Legs Sautéed in Garlic Butter

SERVES 12

Again, this is not the usual cocktail party fare. The thing to do is plan ahead and cut off the legs and freeze them separately from the rest of the bird. Use the breasts in another recipe and just enjoy the legs. They are the most succulent part of the bird. In an unusual switch, woodcock legs are white meat and the breast is dark meat.

If you don't have any woodcock, substitute the upper joint only of chicken wings. They resemble tiny drumsticks. Simmer the leftover wing tips with a little celery and onion to make chicken stock for use in other recipes if you hate to throw anything out, as I do. If you are using chicken, double or triple the recipe below.

Melt the butter and oil in a heavy-bottomed skillet and sauté the garlic for 1 minute, stirring so it won't scorch. Add the woodcock legs and cook for 2 to 3 minutes on each side, turning them once to brown evenly. Don't cook for much more than 5 to 6 minutes in all. Move quickly through the crowd, allowing 1 to each guest and vowing to yourself to get more woodcock next year.

12 woodcock legs
1 clove garlic, put through a
    garlic press
2 tablespoons butter
1 tablespoon oil
Salt and freshly ground white
    pepper to taste

Dove Breasts Wrapped in Bacon

Preheat oven to 375°.

Fillet the breasts and use the remaining parts of the dove to make soup.

Wrap each half breast in a bacon strip, and place in 1 layer in a roasting pan. Cook in the preheated oven for 10 minutes. If the bacon isn't crisp, broil for a minute or two. Put a toothpick in each and serve.

Any number of dove breasts
2 slices bacon for each breast

Pheasant Pâté

SERVES 12—2 OR 3 CANAPES PER PERSON

Preheat oven to 350°.

Salt and pepper the outsides of the birds, and if they have been skinned, place strips of bacon over breasts. Bake in covered roasting pan to which ½ inch water has been added.

Place in preheated oven and cook for 1 to 1½ hours. (You do want the meat to fall off the bones in this case.)

Cool, remove all meat from bones, discard the bones and skin, and cut out any discolored spots caused by shot. Put meat through the fine blade of a meat grinder, or use the metal blade in a food processor to mince finely. Add 1 tablespoon grated onion per pheasant, and 1 finely sieved or chopped hard-boiled egg, and ½ stick melted butter for each 2 pheasants. Mix in enough sour cream to thoroughly moisten the mixture and make it spreadable. Add salt and freshly ground pepper to taste.

Mix well and pack in small tightly closed jars and refrigerate or freeze. When ready to serve, place in a small deep bowl, garnish with a little parsley or watercress, and serve with crackers or toast points.

2 plucked, cleaned, thawed pheasants
Bacon strips
2 tablespoons onion, grated
1 hard-boiled egg
⅛ pound (½ stick) butter, melted
¼ cup sour cream
Salt and freshly ground pepper to taste

"Woods Edge" Caviar and Egg Ring

MAKES 1 RING MOLD

½ pound caviar of your choice
1 dozen hard-boiled eggs
¼ pound (1 stick) butter, melted
2 tablespoons prepared Dijon mustard
1 small onion, minced finely

Finely mince the hard-boiled eggs in a food processor, using the on-off technique and watching like a hawk. Or mash them with a fork. Add the mustard, minced onions, and melted butter, and mix well. Press into a ring mold and chill for at least 3 hours.

When ready to serve, unmold by briefly dipping the mold into hot water and inverting onto a serving plate. Fill the center with the caviar and surround with crackers or toast points.

Cocktail Pissaladettes

MAKES 18 PISSALADETTES
(AMPLE FOR 12 PEOPLE)

One 12-ounce package of 9 French-style rolls
3 medium-sized Spanish onions (Vidalia onions would be delicious if they are available. You'll need about 6.)
3 tablespoons butter
1 tablespoon olive oil
Two 2-ounce cans flat anchovy fillets
½ pound (approximately) Kalamata olives, halved and pitted (Italian black olives can be used, but the flavor isn't the same)
½ pound freshly grated Parmesan cheese

This is a takeoff on a hearty Provençal version of pizza. It can be made in a luncheon-size version by splitting French baguettes lengthwise, cutting them into 8-inch lengths and using the same topping of onions, anchovies, and olives. Another version of it is the Onion Tart (which see).

Preheat oven to 375°.

Peel and slice the onions very thin. Steam them over very low heat in the 1 tablespoon oil and 2 tablespoons butter in a covered heavy-bottomed frying pan. It will take about 25 minutes. The onions should not be browned. They should be golden in color and close to the consistency of jam.

Split or carefully tear the rolls in half lengthwise. Arrange them split side up on a cookie sheet. Sprinkle the Parmesan evenly over the split tops of the rolls. Spread the cooked onions over them. Drain the anchovies on paper towels and arrange 2 fillets in an X on top of the onions. Place the halved, pitted olives in the center of each space between the anchovy crosses.

Place in the preheated oven for 15 to 20 minutes, until the bread is heated through and the onions are piping hot. Serve at once.

APPENDIX

A Brief Manual on How to
Clean, Pluck,
Hang, and Freeze Game,
and How to Cook by the
Internal Temperature Method

by Leigh Perkins

The Meat Thermicator

This is a very precise instrument manufactured by the leading thermocouple-instrument company. The president of that company developed this instrument in cooperation with Orvis for the gourmet game and meat cook, and because of our common interest in game and meat cookery, we have made this sophisticated commercial instrument available to the public. It gives an immediate internal temperature reading of anything the retractable needle is placed in. This is the secret to meat cookery perfection. The needle is less than $\frac{1}{16}$ inch in diameter, minimizing any loss of juice from puncture. The needle is retractable and can be set to the proper depth, so that if one is cooking a steak 1½ inches thick, the needle can be set at ¾ inch.

Although sensitive, this instrument is not delicate. We have tested these instruments for fourteen years, carrying them on canoe trips and in suitcases checked on planes (a real test). If for any reason you doubt the Meat Thermicator's reading, check by placing it in boiling water. If it doesn't read 212° at (approximately) sea level, it can easily be adjusted using the setscrew on the front.

The temperature reading is instantaneous. One can reach over hot coals or into an oven without disturbing the cooking process. The dial reads in degrees Fahrenheit, and it is charted for the proper internal temperature for various game and meat. Even if you are not a game cook, this instrument will save its cost in ruined charcoal-grilled steaks or beef roast in a season or two.

The Art of Cooking Game

Warning: The internal temperatures in this book are based on Meat Thermicator readings. Do not expect the same results with ordinary meat thermometers. Our tests show that meat thermometers will not work at all on small game and invariably read considerably higher than the accurate Meat Thermicator on larger birds and roasts.

Despite motion pictures showing the glamorous heroine ordering pheasant under glass, or champagne and quail, there has been a fairly universal misconception by hunters' helpmates that wild things are unclean, strong of odor, and generally unpleasant as table fare. Cookbooks have taken this attitude into account and in recipes for wild duck and other game have lavished pages on recipes for game that require hours for preparation. Usually the recipe involves a marinade and an elaborate sauce. This means the hunter's cook must start the day before or at least in the early morning of the day of the game dinner. At best it is an ordeal.

The typical game recipe almost always finishes by saying "roast until tender," and the cook takes this to mean "cook the hell out of it." Whatever she would have done to pot roast, she will do to game. Hers is a reasonable assumption, because after passing the critical internal temperature of between 120° and 150°, all meat gets tougher and tougher until it reaches the totally flavorless stage at 190° when it falls off the bones.

Cooking game is much like cooking a soft-boiled egg. There is a critical degree of internal temperature. One can arrive at it by calculating time, temperature, and thickness or weight of meat. There is one major problem in this method—temperature. When charcoal broiling, oven broiling, or pan frying it is difficult to tell the temperature. Roasting can also be misleading. Oven thermostats are often 75 degrees off. In almost every home oven there are hot and not-so-hot areas. Of two ducks, both 1½ pounds, placed in the same oven, one can come out well done and one medium.

The real crux of the matter is the internal temperature of the meat. It is somewhat significant how the meat arrives at the proper temperature, and there are degrees of preference. One can cook certain birds at a high temperature (450°) for a short time, for instance eleven minutes for quail and nineteen minutes for a mallard duck. Or one can use a lower temperature (350°) for a longer time, forty-five minutes for pheasant, for instance.

There are reasons for this difference in approach. Duck is fat and self-basting and can stand a high temperature. Some people prefer it rare, equivalent to rare steak, (internal temperature 120°). One hundred thirty to one hundred forty degrees gives you a medium-rare bird—firm meat all the way through with a deep pink center. Anything over this is overdone and on the way to being tough and flavorless.

The internal temperature range of cooked quail should be 130° to 150°. The quail is small enough so that in eleven minutes the outside will not dry out. High heat for a short time seals in juices.

On the other hand, pheasant, wild turkey, and ruffed grouse have very little fat and require a slower cooking time. With these birds the ideal oven temperature is 350°.

Dark-meat birds such as duck and woodcock have muscles designed for long duration flights. These migratory birds tend to get tough and unpalatable above 150°.

White-meat birds—quail, ruffed grouse, pheasant—have high-energy muscles for short duration flights. These birds can rarely sustain flights of over one mile. Ideal internal temperature is 130° to 150°. Our preference is 140°, which produces a firm but moist center. Cooked to a temperature of 150° the bird is still tender but a little more firm. Over 150° internal temperature all game birds begin to get tough and flavorless and are a loss, except as the base for some fancy sauce.

A Brief Game Primer

DOVE

It is best to hang doves under refrigeration for 4 days in the feathers. (Hanging ideally means hanging by the neck in a cooler, but they can simply be placed on a refrigerator shelf.) They are almost as good if you want to eat them immediately, but they tend to be a little tougher 12 to 48 hours after killing them. It is not necessary to draw the birds until after hanging and plucking.

Plucking: The dove is very easy to pluck because it has loose feathers and firm skin. They pluck well on a mechanical duck plucker. If you hunt early in the season, the bird may be covered with pin feathers almost impossible to pluck. Don't worry—leave the pin feathers on while cooking and skin the bird before serving. Place the crisp bacon you have basted it with back on top of the bird before arranging on a serving platter.

Freezing: Dove may be frozen in water. Put 6 or 7 in a 1-quart plastic container, fill with water, and freeze. Frozen birds are not as good as fresh-hung and should not be kept more than 5 to 6 months.

Roasting: Roasting time should be 8 to 10 minutes. The internal temperature should be 130° to 150°. At 130° the center will be deep pink. At 140° (our preference) the center will be light pink. At 150° the center will be brown all the way through but still moist and good. Plan 2 doves per serving for small appetites.

DUCK

There have probably been more of these wonderful birds brought home with pride and then ruined in the kitchen than any other bird. If anyone says he likes duck well done, you know right away he would rather have hamburger, and that is what we suggest you serve him.

Ducks present some new and interesting problems because the duck's diets can affect the flavor. This should not eliminate them as table birds, but they do require varied preparations. Mallard, black duck, pintail, widgeon, teal (all types), shoveler, wood duck, canvasback, redhead, and ring-necked duck are always excellent and should be prepared in the regular way.

The following ducks can be just as good at times, but at other times they include fish and shellfish in their diets, which can affect their flavor: greater and lesser scaup, hooded merganser, ruddy duck, and bufflehead. As for gadwall, this guy is a special case. Ninety-nine percent of the time he is just as good as mallard, but once in a while he will eat something that affects his flavor, and about this you need have no doubt—when you clean him you will know right away and no one will have to tell you to throw him out.

Once I shot 3 gadwall during the same hour in the same place. Two were excellent and one no good. Give them the benefit of the doubt until cleaning.

Ducks that always have a problem are golden eye, American merganser, red merganser, old squaw, and scoter. Now for the good ducks.

Preparation: Hang them in their feathers, head up, in a refrigerator or cooler for 4 to 6 days. It is not necessary to draw ducks before hanging unless they are badly gut-shot.

Plucking: First, with anvil-knife-type pruning shears cut wings and head off as near the body as possible. Cut 1 leg off just above the joint (leave the other on as a handle for the following process).

If plucking by hand, take most of the outer feathers off back, flanks, and tail. Prepare a 2-gallon bucket (not plastic) by filling ½ full of water adding ¼ pound paraffin for each duck to be cleaned. Boil the water until the paraffin is melted. Let cool about 10 minutes.

Now submerge the duck in the bucket so that when it is pulled out the feathers and down are totally coated with paraffin. Lay on a newspaper for 5 minutes to cool. At this stage it should be simply a matter of peeling off wax, feathers, and down together, just like peeling a tangerine.

If you have an electric duck plucker, leave all appendages on until after plucking on the machine for 1 minute.

Cleaning: Cut a large opening in the rear vent. The crop and windpipe may be removed from the front—pull everything else out through the rear cavity. Save heart and liver for sautéing or making duck liver pâté.

Freezing: First, it is not recommended to freeze any of the ducks that may have fed on fish or crustaceans. They are perfectly good fresh, but often become strong or rancid when frozen.

The mallard, wood duck, and teal group will last up to 8 months if frozen in water in quart containers or bags. Most ducks fit snugly into a quart freezer bag (not the zip type), and frozen by this method will retain their flavor for 5 months.

Roasting: Preheat oven to 450°. Place duck in open pan with a splash of water and cook until Meat Thermicator indicates 120° to 140°. At 120° the meat is moist and tender, red but firm. At 130° the meat is deep pink like medium-rare steak (our preference). 140° produces a pale pink meat similar to medium steak.

To prepare and cook the scaup, hooded merganser, ruddy duck, and bufflehead, draw before hanging and roast immediately after hanging. An alternate method that is foolproof is to fillet the ducks after plucking, remove skin and all fat, and sauté for approximately 4 minutes on a side until the internal temperature is between 120° and 140°.

For scoter, old squaw, golden eye, American and red-breasted mergansers, we only recommend filleting and sautéing when birds are fresh, before hanging. Prepared this way they are surprisingly delicious. Do not attempt to make duck soup from these ducks' carcasses.

Some approximate oven times: mallard, black canvas back—19–21 minutes; redhead, greater scaup, pintail, gadwall drake—17–19 minutes; wood duck, ring-necked duck, lesser scaup, gadwall hen, widgeon, hooded merganser, shoveler—14–17 minutes; teal, bufflehead, ruddy duck—13–15 minutes.

Preparing for Table: If you have a hearty bunch, serve each person a whole duck. Preferably, fillet the duck and serve fillets with skin on, unless the pinfeather condition makes it more appetizing to remove skin. To fillet, use a sharp knife, preferably with rounded point, and cut down next to breastbone, staying as close to bone structure as possible. Make a second cut under wing and leg, taking as much meat as possible to meet the first cut. If one tries to do it all in 1 cut, much meat will be missed. Most people will find the fillets more appetizing than the whole duck. This way, only the breast is served. The rest of the carcass contains much meat that is difficult to get at and the legs are quite tough. We recommend pressing the jucies in a duck press, or making Duck Soup from the carcasses.

Another way to prepare wild duck fillets is to fillet the ducks as described above, then remove the skin and sauté 5 minutes on each side on very low heat. The internal temperature should be 130° to 140°. The fillets will be an appetizing brown with the center only slightly pink. Jessie Hill, the greatest game cook I know, figured this method out to initiate the newcomer to the delights of wild duck.

A close friend of mine was having a big dinner for a large number of VIPs and had collected some 18 wild ducks. The south Georgia farmhand who was commissioned to pluck the ducks had heard about some shortcut, dipping the duck in "parafeen." Unfortunately over the telephone, paraffin was interpreted as kerosene. Eighteen ducks were buried, and I believe the VIPs ate ham that evening. Old proverb: There are lots of ways to ruin a wild duck.

GOOSE

Wild geese have the reputation of being tough, dry, and rather inferior table fare. This is absolutely right if you follow the typical goose or poultry recipe.

There is great variation in geese as to age and weight. Geese should be drawn and hung under refrigeration or outside at 40° to 50° for 5 to 7 days, in the feathers.

Pluck and prepare as for duck, except allow 2 pounds of paraffin for each goose. They pluck well on a mechanical duck plucker but it is necessary to singe the small hairlike feathers off afterward.

Place in open roasting pan with ½ cup water. Place in an oven preheated to 350° for approximately 12 minutes per pound. Internal temperature should be 130° to 140° when done. The goose will be tender and moist at 130°, firmer and drier at 140°.

Geese may be frozen in freezer paper but we do not recommend keeping them more than 5 months.

OCTOPUS

To clean, cut off the tentacles between the eye and the beak. Save them. Squeeze out the beak between your thumb and forefinger and discard it. Hold the blade of a large knife almost flat against the body and scrape toward the open end of the body cavity. (If you cut through the skin, move the blade closer to parallel to the body.) Turn the body over and repeat this procedure. By now all of the entrails should be squeezed out. Dispose of them. If you can feel any remaining entrails in the body, remove by hand or spoon.

If you are using squid, stab the transparent quill that protrudes from the body with a knife and hold it fast. Pull the body away. The quill should remain under the knife—discard it.

Cut the body and tentacles across to make rings—½ inch is a good size for the recipe in Chapter 5.

PARTRIDGE OR RUFFED GROUSE

The ruffed grouse is considered by us to be the greatest of delicacies. Of all the gallinaceous birds common in the United States, this bird has a far different diet from the others. Its food consists mostly of berries, greens, fruit, and buds. Grouse eat very little grain. This diet produces a flavor all its own.

Grouse should be hung under refrigeration at 40° to 50° for 4 to 6 days. They should be drawn before hanging. Liver and heart are small but excellent sautéed or made into pâté and spread on toast under the cooked bird.

Preparing: This is probably the most difficult bird to pluck because the skin is very tender. The only method is to dry-pluck. One must be patient and pluck feathers a few at a time, especially around the breast, or the skin will tear. It is difficult to avoid a few tears and one should not despair if this occurs.

There is little meat on the wings and they should be clipped off at the first joint.

Freezing Grouse: In the past we have frozen grouse, after hanging and preparing, in a quart plastic container filled with water. Recently we learned from hunting companion Bill Cheney of freezing in the feathers. We have tested this against freezing in water and find it superior.

The grouse must be drawn and hung 4 to 6 days. Clip the head and neck off and pull tail feathers. Clip legs off at the first joint. Leave wings on, but trim off about 2 inches of primary feathers. Fold wings tight against the body and slip breast into a 1-quart plastic freezer bag (not zip type). Grouse should fit snugly with just enough room to tie off with a twistie. Press out all air when sealing. Birds will last 6 to 8 months this way with no loss of flavor. When plucking after freezing, let thaw about 1 hour, then pluck. The meat is still frozen but the skin has thawed and plucking is relatively easy.

Roasting: Place birds in an open pan, breast up, with a splash of water. Place 3 half strips of bacon over each breast and put in preheated 350° oven for 35 minutes, approximately. Internal temperaturee is critical and should be 130° to 150° when done. The breast is the whole show because the legs are quite stringy.

PHEASANT

Hang 5 or 6 days under refrigeration. The skin and feathers are similar to a chicken's. The skin is reasonably firm and pheasant can be dry-plucked or dipped in scalding water and wet-plucked. Pheasant does not pluck well on a mechanical duck plucker. Clip off wings at first joint, legs at joint, and neck close to body. Pheasant may be frozen in feathers as described under grouse, only use ½-gallon freezer bags. Liver and heart may be sautéed or used in pâté.

Roasting: Place in open pan with splash of water, breast up. Cover breast with 4 full strips of bacon. Place in a preheated 350° oven for 35 to 50 minutes, depending on size. Test with Meat Thermicator. Internal temperature should be 130° to 150° when done. We recommend 140° for best flavor and moistness.

QUAIL

It is best to hang quail under refrigeration for 4 days in the feathers.

Plucking: There is no shortcut if you don't have a duck plucker. Quail skin is tender and if you try to pull off too many feathers at a time you will tear the skin. After a little practice one should be able to prepare a bird in about 5 minutes. It is worth the effort because without the skin the birds dry out during cooking.

Cleaning: Snip off legs just above joint. Wings can be trimmed right to the body because there is very little meat on them and they are difficult to pluck. Trim the neck right to the body. I find the knife-anvil pruning shears work better for this than game shears. To clean, enlarge opening at rear vent and clean out insides. The crop can be removed from the neck cavity. The crop is a little food-storage pouch and pulls right out. Discard it. Wash, clean, and dry bird. Save the heart and liver. They don't amount not much in size but they are delicious sautéed on toast, or if you have enough (at least ½ cup), you can make a wonderful quail liver pâté.

Freezing: Preferably, freeze in water-filled heavy plastic containers available at hardware stores or freezer plants. Birds will last up to 9 months this way. If frozen in freezer paper or baggies, we recommend eating within 5 to 6 months.

SNIPE

Hang for 4 days. Prepare as for quail, except snipe is a delight to pluck because the feathers come off very easily and the skin is very firm. If early in the season, the bird may be heavily pinfeathered. Again, don't bother with them; cook in pinfeathers and skin before serving. Often, even on cleaned birds, there will be some very fine hairlike feathers left. These can readily be singed off over an open flame. We do not recommend freezing snipe for more than 6 weeks, and they are far better not frozen at all.

Roasting: Place the whole cleaned bird in a pan breast side up with just a splash of water to moisten the bottom of the pan. Place in a 475° oven for 10 minutes. The internal temperature should reach 130° to 150°.

Broiling or Charcoal Broiling: Split down the breast, not the back, with game shears. Broil 4 minutes on a side maximum. Snipe are very rich in spite of their small size. Two per person will normally suffice. For the especially adventurous, snipe can be cooked and eaten with the innards. We prefer snipe to woodcock this way because it is possible to cook the innards properly with the smaller birds without ruining the breast by overcooking. When cooking with the innards, set the oven at 400° and cook for approximately 15 minutes. Check with the Meat Thermicator. It should be 130° to 150° internal temperature, depending on how rare you like your bird.

VENISON

Preparing: Be sure to skin the deer the day it was killed or as soon as possible. Hang the carcass 10 days to 2 weeks whole or in quarters in a meat locker. It is best to have a professional butcher cut up the meat after hanging and vacuum-package for freezing.

Venison Liver: Many consider the liver the choicest part of the deer. The slicing of the liver is as important as the cooking. With a sharp knife slice across the liver so the pieces are 1 inch thick when possible. Thin slices are bound to overcook. Sauté slices in butter over low heat until internal temperature is 120° to 140°. To retain flavor and tenderness the center of a liver strip must be deep pink (130°) to light pink (140°).

Venison Chops and Steaks: To retain flavor and tenderness, venison must be cooked rare to medium-rare. Internal temperature should reach 120° to 140°. Sauté, grill, or broil as you would any steak or chop. Make sure chops and steaks are cut thick, preferably at least 1 inch.

The best of all is the tenderloin or backstrap. One sacrifices loin chops to take the whole loin, but we think it is worth it. The loin is only 2 to 3 inches in diameter and should be roasted at 350° for 25 to 30 minutes. The internal temperature should be 120° to 140°. The loin is equally good sliced down and across the grain, 1½ inches thick, and grilled.

WILD TURKEY

Wild turkey has the same problem as pheasant—they're dry and can easily be overcooked—and most of us don't get enough of them with which to experiment. We can assure you that if you place a wild turkey in an oven and follow directions for most domestic turkey, that is, cook until the internal temperature is 185°, you will have only a very poor base for gravy and cranberry sauce.

Wild turkey should be drawn first and hung 7 to 9 days in a cooler at 40° to 50°. Pluck after hanging, either dry (easier than you think), or dip in scalding water and wet-pluck. If frozen in freezer paper, we recommend eating within

5 to 6 months. (With our next turkey we will try freezing in the feathers as described for grouse.)

Roasting: Place the wild turkey in a roasting pan with enough strips of bacon to cover breast. The turkey should be approximately room temperature before placing in the oven. Add 1 cup of water to roasting pan. Roast in preheated 350° oven for 10 minutes per pound and test with Meat Thermicator. Internal temperature should be 140° to 150°.

Note: We recommend leaving the cover off the roasting pan. At 140° to 150° internal temperature the turkey will be done through but firm and easy to carve. The meat will not fall apart but will be moist and have a distinct flavor not found in domestic turkey.

WOODCOCK

Hang for 4 days. Pluck as for snipe. Woodcock are much like snipe as table fare, only larger and with a lighter coating of fat. Prepare in the same manner as for snipe.

We do not recommend freezing woodcock, but if you do, eat it within 6 weeks.

Roasting: Place in a preheated 450° oven for 12 to 14 minutes. Test with the Meat Thermicator. It should be from 130° to 150° internal temperature, depending on preference for doneness.

Broiling or Charcoal Broiling: Split bird down middle of breast. Otherwise, the woodcock would be impossible to flatten. No basting is necessary. Normally, about 5 minutes on each side is sufficient, but test earlier with the Meat Thermicator. Internal temperature should reach 130° to 150°. Warning: This bird will get tough if overcooked.

If you want to go the whole way with woodcock, eat him insides and all. First, have 3 martinis and second, cook more slowly. Follow the same roasting procedure, but use a 350° oven for 25 minutes. Test with the Meat Thermicator—the innards should get up to at least 125°. Remember, the heart, liver and little white coil of intestine are all good, but the craw is not. Don't look for a gizzard, because there is none.

INDEX